ACADEMIC AIDS, INC.
An Educational Store For Teachers & Parents
206-537-6270
11012 Canyon Rd. E., Suite #19
Puyallup, WA 98373

The KIDS' STUFF™ Book of
MATH
For The Middle Grades

by
Marjorie Frank

illustrated by Kathleen Bullock

Incentive Publications, Inc.
Nashville, Tennessee

Illustrated by Kathleen Bullock
Cover by Susan Eaddy
Edited by Sally Sharpe

ISBN 0-86530-012-7

Copyright © 1988 by Incentive Publications, Inc., Nashville, Tennessee. All rights reserved. No part of this publication may be reproduced, stored in a retrieval system, or transmitted in any form or by any means (electronic, mechanical, photocopying, recording, or otherwise) without prior written permission of Incentive Publications, Inc., with the exception below.

All pages labeled as student pages and the pages in the appendix, Math Tools & Treasures, are intended for reproduction. Permission is hereby granted to the purchaser to reproduce these pages in quantities suitable for meeting yearly student needs.

TABLE OF CONTENTS

FRACTIONS & DECIMALS

RATIO, PROPORTION, & PERCENT

MEASUREMENT

GEOMETRY

PROBABILITY, STATISTICS, & GRAPHING

WELCOME TO MIDDLE GRADES MATH . . .

The world of the middle grades student is full of math. Math can be found hiding in the lunchroom and the gymnasium, in backpacks and lockers, in backyards and even in music! Every day the middle grader's life is filled with things that need to be measured, calculated or deciphered with mathematical skills.

Math is fun and challenging for kids in the "middle ages." Both in and out of the classroom, math is a marvelous means for developing minds by stretching reasoning abilities. What's more, math builds excitement and curiosity about the wonderful world that is unfolding to these "almost-grown-up" persons.

THE KIDS' STUFF™ BOOK OF MATH FOR THE MIDDLE GRADES was created just for students of this age. Its purpose is to capture the interest and imaginations of students and to promote growth of specific math skills needed for successful living.

This book was also created for you, the middle grades teacher. Each chapter division contains teacher pages (lessons that require very little advance preparation) and reproducible student pages (ready-to-use activities which require minimal teacher direction). For your convenience, every activity is grouped according to a major math area of the middle grades curriculum. In addition, every page is clearly labeled with the emphasized skill.

Furthermore, a generous appendix has been included especially for the busy middle grades teacher (Math Tools And Treasures). This section has everything you need for teaching math —formulas, symbols, measurement tables, metric conversions and the most complete glossary of math terms and items you've ever seen!

You'll find this book to be a handy tool to have at your finger tips. There are enough extra puzzles, investigations, and challenges to supplement your basic math program all year long!

Marjorie Frank

HOW TO USE THIS BOOK . . .

THE KIDS' STUFF™ BOOK OF MATH FOR THE MIDDLE GRADES is loaded with the kinds of "extras" that enrich basic middle grades math programs. This book also contains thoroughly outlined lessons. These lessons introduce and reinforce solid, basic skills. You'll find plenty of ideas for teaching a concept, presenting a unit, or motivating involvement in a new area of math. On some days, this resource will be a wonderful break from the textbook. On other days it will be the textbook's best companion!

Begin by familiarizing yourself with the chapter contents. In the table of contents, each activity is labeled by skill. When you are in need of a lesson plan or a math exercise for your students, simply choose one suited to the skill you are studying.

The 🍎 symbol identifies the teacher pages. Each of these pages outlines a plan for you to follow in presenting a teacher-directed math activity to the class. Quite often a student page accompanies a teacher page so that the concept may be strengthened by student practice.

The student pages, labeled with a ✏️ symbol, invite students to investigate a problem or complete an interesting task. These pages are not "busywork" but are work sheets intended to be used with teacher direction — often as an integral part of a lesson you present. Once underway, however, the student pages may be completed on an individual basis with little teacher involvement.

The appendix, Math Tools and Treasures, may be used as a reference section for you and your students. You will find the many tables, formulas, and listings helpful for individual student use.

At the end of this book is an answer section which includes solutions to "tricky" problems. Of course, activities having a variety of possible answers are not included in this section.

- You have permission to reproduce pages labeled as student pages and pages included in the Math Tools and Treasures appendix.

NUMBER CONCEPTS

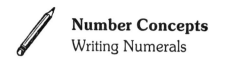

Name _____

SKYWRITERS

What is the name of each numeral being written by the skywriters?

Write the words beside each numeral.

1. **8,649** _____.

2. **4.55** _____.

3. **99,999** _____.

4. **8** _____.

5. **7/8** _____.

6. **2,400,560** _____.

_____.

Now, you write the numerals. Use a large piece of drawing paper if you like on which to write each one in "skywriting."

7. thirty thousand, three hundred _____

8. six tenths _____

9. five and three hundredths _____

10. five and three tenths _____

11. nine hundred thousand _____

12. four elevenths _____

13. six million, twenty thousand, five _____

14. eighty-three thousandths _____

15. ten and four hundredths _____

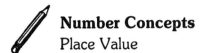

Name _____

NAME THAT PLACE !

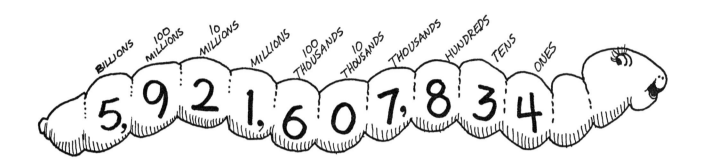

Review the value of each place from the ones place to the billions place.

For each number below, write the value or name of the place where the worm has stopped to munch.

(1.) 39<u>7</u>,059 _____

(2) 79,500,<u>9</u>18 _____

(3.) <u>1</u>0,000,000,000 _____

(4.) 9<u>7</u>04 _____

(5.) 50,<u>8</u>86,930 _____

(6.) 1<u>7</u>,974,303,999 _____

(7.) 26<u>0</u> _____

(8.) 66<u>6</u>,666,666,666 _____

(9.) 5<u>8</u>0,977 _____

(10.) 8<u>6</u>4,900,533 _____

AIM FOR A BULL'S-EYE

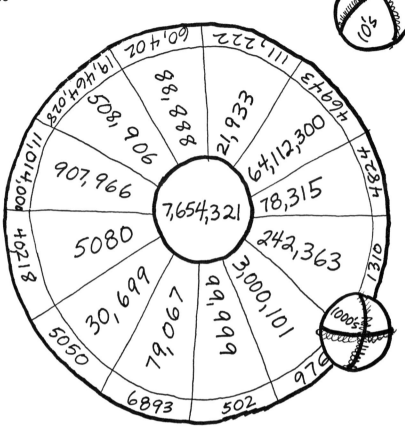

Preparation:

- Have a group of students make a dart board by drawing circles with permanent markers on a large square of colored felt.
- Write several numerals on the circles, such as:

508,906	5080	79,067	3,000,100
907,966	30,906	99,999	7,063,864

- Glue two to three strips of Velcro on each of nine ping pong balls.
- Use permanent markers to write the following words on the balls:

tens	hundreds	thousands
ten thousands	hundred thousands	millions
ten millions	hundred millions	billions

Use:

1) Have students practice rounding whole numbers by playing this dart game.
   - Choose a ball with your eyes closed.
   - Toss the ball at the dart board.
   - Round the number closest to where the ball lands to the nearest place indicated on the ball.

2) A partner may verify correct rounding. Each player may collect a point for each correct answer. A bull's-eye is worth 10 points.

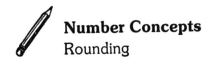

Name _____

ROUND 'EM UP!

ROUNDUP RULES

If a digit is 5 or higher, round it UP.
If it is less than 5, round DOWN.

Follow the directions inside each lasso to help the cowboy finish the roundup.

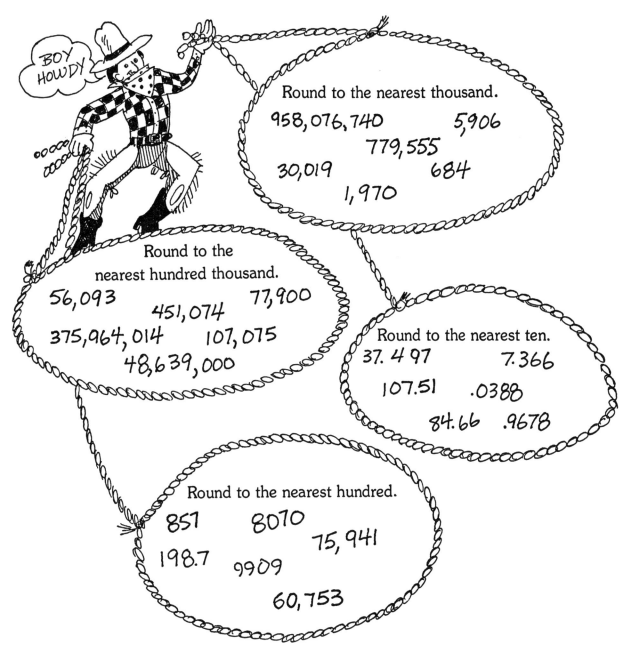

Round to the nearest thousand.
958,076,740   5,906
779,555
30,019   684
1,970

Round to the
nearest hundred thousand.
56,093   77,900
451,074
375,964,014   107,075
48,639,000

Round to the nearest ten.
37. 4 97   7.366
107.51   .0388
84.66   .9678

Round to the nearest hundred.
857   8070
75,941
198.7   9909
60,753

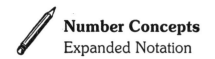

Number Concepts
Expanded Notation

Name _____

NUMBERS THAT BALLOON

You can "stretch out" any numeral or "make it balloon" to show what each digit in the numeral means. This is called expanded notation.

Help these kids "blow up" the numerals below. Write each numeral in expanded notation.

Example: 430,709 = 400,000 + 30,000 + 700 + 9

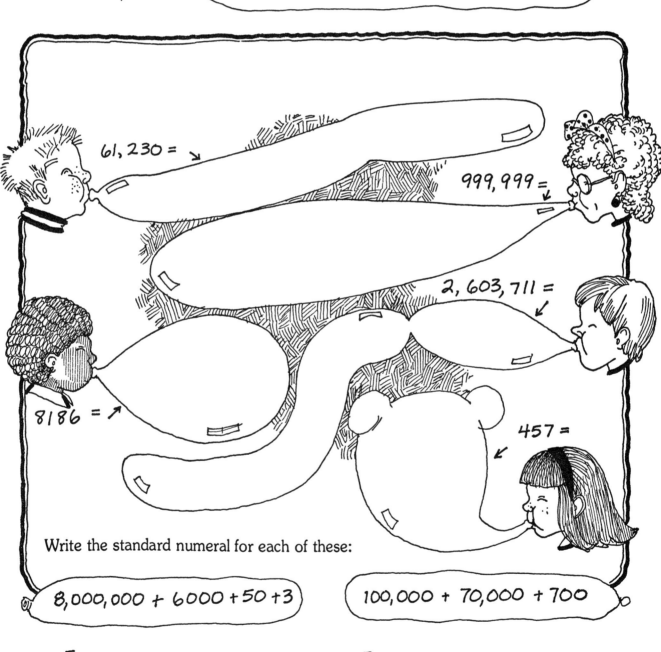

61,230 =

999,999 =

2,603,711 =

8186 =

457 =

Write the standard numeral for each of these:

8,000,000 + 6000 + 50 + 3

100,000 + 70,000 + 700

= _____

= _____

Student Page

16

Name _____

ORDER IN THE COURT

Judge Samantha Stern is calling her courtroom to order. (You can see that it's in a terrible disarray.) You have five minutes to get all of the persons in the room in order — or else you'll be in contempt of court!

Write the numbers in sequential order down the side of the page.

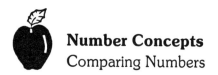

Number Concepts
Comparing Numbers

ORDER, PLEASE!

Preparation:

- Use a marker to write the following numbers on paper plates.

3,597	.0467	1.496	5,000,011	5,010,011
4.074	77	999	780,501	333,003
2,900	1000.5	1000	303,333	1,000,000
5.957	5.9577	6196.5	6197	803.333
.0986	.15966	37.666	805.07	309.5644
.0996	309.7	507.96	6,000,000	30.9001

(You may substitute whole numbers for decimals if students are inexperienced with decimals.)

- String each plate with yarn so that it may be hung around a student's neck.

Use:

1) Have each student "wear" a numeral.
2) Divide the class into groups of approximately five students. Instruct each group to place itself in order from the lowest to highest number.
3) Have the groups combine to form one long line of numbers arranged from the lowest to highest number.
4) Instruct each student to write any numeral, whole number or decimal, on the blank side of his or her plate. Now repeat the activity.

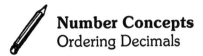

Number Concepts
Ordering Decimals

Name _____

RIDE THE CREST

Help the surfer ride the wave without falling off the surf board by putting each group of decimals in the correct order from lowest to highest value. Write the smallest value at the bottom of the wave and the largest value at the top.

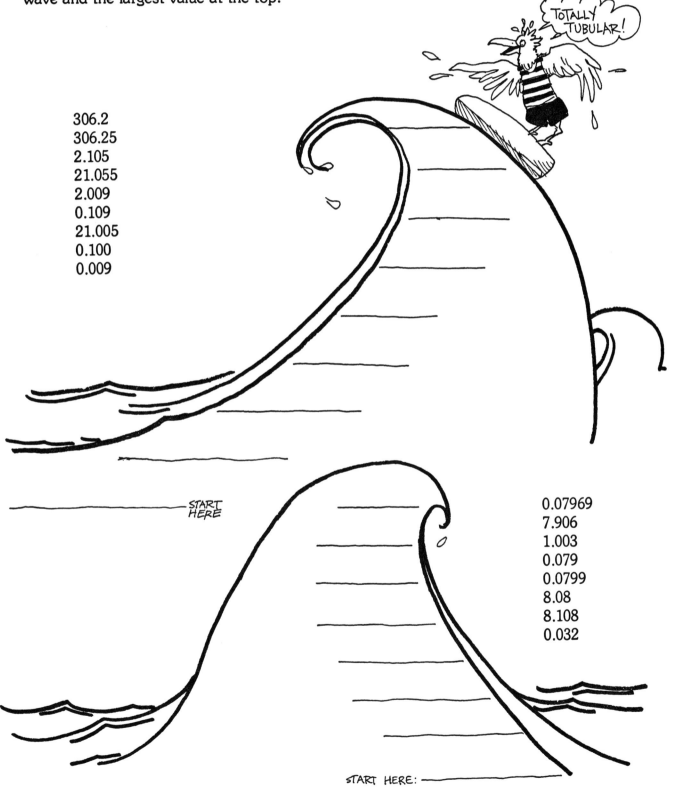

306.2
306.25
2.105
21.055
2.009
0.109
21.005
0.100
0.009

START HERE

0.07969
7.906
1.003
0.079
0.0799
8.08
8.108
0.032

START HERE:

Answers on page 238.

Student Page

PROPERTY FOR SALE

Preparation:
- Have a group of students make large charts of number properties "for sale," using the pictures below as examples.

Use:
1) Place the property charts at the front of the room. Discuss together each of the four properties of multiplication and addition.
2) Give each student a copy of the student page "Property Shopping." Have students match each property for sale with the correct property represented by the number sentence written on the home.

COMMUTATIVE PROPERTY

Changing the order of addends or factors does not change the sum or product.

$$3 + 5 = 5 + 3$$

$$2 \times 6 = 6 \times 2$$

ASSOCIATIVE PROPERTY

Changing the grouping of addends or factors does not change the sum or product.

$$(4 + 2) + 10 = 4 + (2 + 10)$$
$$(7 \times 3) \times 4 = 7 \times (3 \times 4)$$

DISTRIBUTIVE PROPERTY

Multiplying a sum by a number is the same as multiplying each addend by the number and adding the two products together.

$$6 \times 57 = (6 \times 50) + (6 \times 7)$$
or
$$6 \times (50 + 7) = (6 \times 50) + (6 \times 7)$$

PROPERTY OF ONE

Any number multiplied by 1 is equal to the original number.

$$45 \times 1 = 45$$

Name _____

PROPERTY SHOPPING

Which number property is represented by each "property for sale" below? Write the correct property (commutative, associative, distributive, or property of one) by each "home."

A. $9 \times (3+6) = (9 \times 3) + (9 \times 6)$

B. $5 \times (3+2) = 5 \times 5$

C. $4 \times (6 \times 2) = (4 \times 6) \times 2$

D. $64 \times 1 = 64$

E. $1 \times 9999 = 9999 \times 1$

F. $86 \times 33 = 33 \times 86$

G. $7 + 4 = 4 + 7$

H. $(8+12)+6 = 8+(12+6)$

READY FOR PRIME TIME

Preparation:

- Make two large T.V. screens from poster board or cardboard. (Students can do this for you!)
- Write an explanation of prime numbers and composites on two rectangular signs.
- Attach the T.V. screens, with a sign above each, to a bulletin board or the front chalkboard.

Use:

1) Discuss the definitions of prime and composite numbers with the class. Remind students that 0 and 1 are neither.
2) Write several numbers on the board. Ask students to work in pairs to decide which numbers are "ready for prime time" (are prime numbers).
3) Let each pair write a few prime numbers on the "PRIME TIME" screen and few composites on the "NOT PRIME TIME" screen.

- Ask students to list all prime numbers under 100. (They should list 25.)

Name _____

THE MYSTERY PLACE

Determine the value of each digit place marked by an arrow. Write your answers on the number cards.

.1 3 6 5 9 7

← TENTHS
← HUNDREDTHS
← THOUSANDTHS
← 10 THOUSANDTHS
← 100 THOUSANDTHS
← MILLIONTHS

MYSTERIES OF MISSING VALUES

1.
↓
1.097

2.
↓
77.980944

3.
↓
18.007957

4.
↓
.00097

5.
↓
265.180

6.
↓
0.7095

7.
↓
8.033

8.
↓
.11183

9.
↓
3.7864

10.
↓
.999999

Number Concepts
Estimation

EDUCATED GUESSES

Preparation:
- Gather these materials:
    large jar of peanut butter
    five table knives
    box of crackers

Use:
1) Spread two crackers with peanut butter for each student. (Students may help!) Allow the students to eat their crackers!
2) Note how much of the peanut butter has been used. Read the weight on the jar.
    - Have the class determine approximately how many ounces of peanut butter each student ate.
    - Tell the students that you would like to buy enough peanut butter to feed five crackers to 100 kids. Discuss how you could estimate the amount of peanut butter and crackers needed for such a task.
    - Record any calculations done to show how you arrived at an "educated guess."

3) Give each student a copy of the following student page, "Guessing Smart," and work together to come up with an estimate for the first two tasks. Record the calculations done to make an educated guess. Have students finish the tasks on their own or in small groups.

Name _____

GUESSING SMART

Write an educated guess for each of these questions.
Show any calculations you've done to arrive at your guess.

A. How many students are there in your school?

B. How long would it take for your entire class to get drinks at the water fountain?

C. 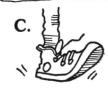 What is the approximate distance that you walk while at school each day?

D. If your whole school (including teachers) ate popcorn during a one-hour movie, how much popcorn (in cups) would be eaten?

E. How many shoelaces would it take to make a string long enough to go all the way around your classroom?

F. How many television programs are watched in a week by all of the kids in your grade at your school?

Student Page

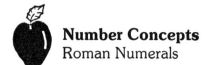

DO AS THE ROMANS DO

Preparation:
- Make a copy of the student page "How the Romans Did It" for each student.

Use:
1) Discuss the Roman numeral system with students.
2) Explain how the Roman numeral system uses addition and subtraction to write symbols for numbers other than 1, 5, 10, 100, 500, and 1000.
3) Practice writing some numbers together, particularly the "tricky" ones such as those below.

400   999   44   1900

4) Let pairs of students work together to write the following in Roman numerals:

> *today's date*
> *year of each student's birth*
> *each student's age*
> *year that each student was five*
> *number of classrooms in the school*
> *year the school was built*
> *answer to 195,077 - 193,206*
> *date of America's independence*
> *total of all the ages in the classroom*
> *date of principal's birth*

5) Check these answers together, then ask students to write the numerals for the problems at the bottom of the following student page.

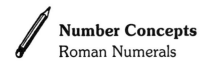

Name _____

HOW THE ROMANS DID IT

Remember: If a larger Roman numeral follows a smaller Roman numeral, subtract.
If a smaller Roman numeral follows a larger Roman numeral, add.

Write the number for each Roman numeral.

1. LXI   2. CDI   3. CLXVIII
4. MXXVI   5. XIX   6. MMDCXCIV

Write a Roman numeral for each of these numbers.

7. 1950   8. 54   9. 3996
10. 499   11. 87   12. 3498

Answers on page 238.

Student Page

EXTRA-TERRESTRIAL EXPONENTS

Preparation:
- Use poster board to make a large UFO. Write the number 64,000,000 miles on it and hang it near the front of the room.
- Make (and hang) 14 additional UFOs. You may wish to use the UFO pattern on the following page. On each UFO, write one of these numbers with a broad-tipped marker.

8000	27,000	4	7	5	3
10,000,000	100	9	10	11	13
100,000,000	1000				

Note: Students might enjoy helping to make the UFOs!

Use:
1) Tell the class that the UFO has arrived from a place 64,000,000 miles away. Show another way of writing this large number — 20^6.
2) Explain exponents. (An exponent shows the number of times a base number — in this case 20 — is used as a factor.) Show the students how to read exponential numbers (twenty to the sixth power).
3) Use the other UFOs for practice in writing a large number as an exponential number and in showing an exponential number as the value of the products.

Teacher Page

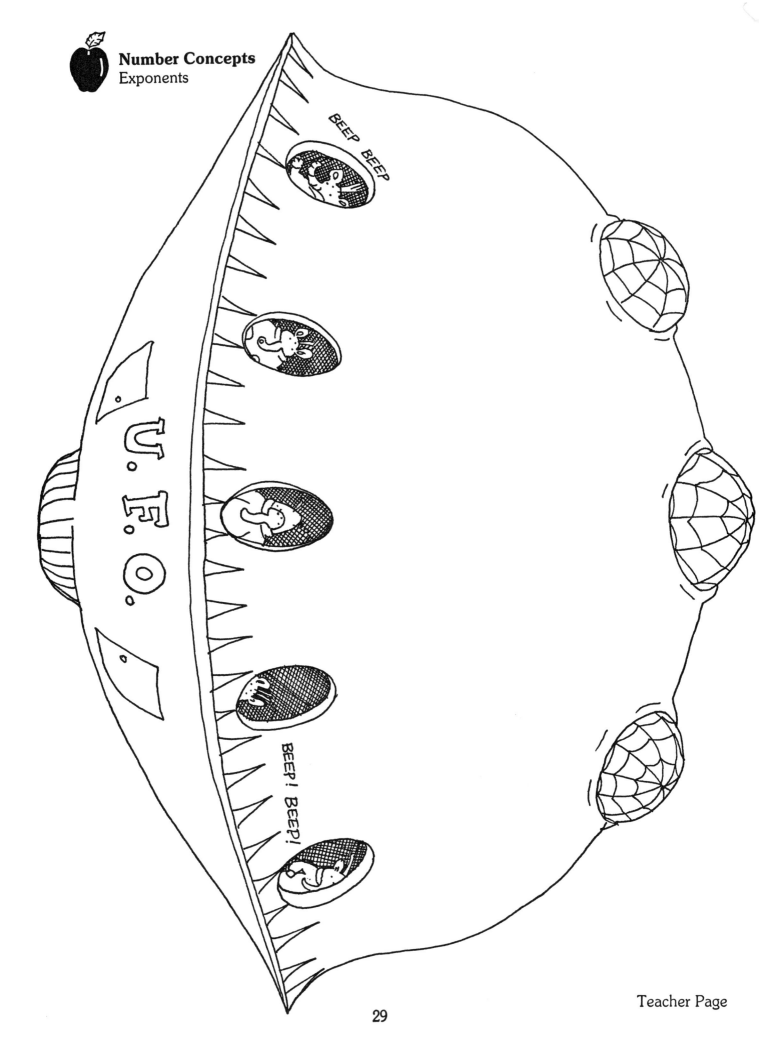

Number Concepts
Divisibility

RULES OF DIVISIBILITY

Preparation:
- Make copies of the student page "Divide and Conquer" for your students.
- Write each of the following numbers on a magician's hat made from black poster board or construction paper. Hang or post the hats around the room.

2000	36	17,144	99	584
7562	8584	128	3005	954
7095	19,557	9843	892	10,340

- Have students make seven rabbits, each labeled with one of these numbers: 2, 3, 4, 5, 8, 9, 10. Hang the rabbits in the front of the room.

Use:
1) Discuss the meaning of "divisibility" with students. Hand out the student page containing the rules for divisibility by various numbers.
2) Practice using the rules to divide several random numbers. Then let students work individually to decide which rabbits go with which hats. (Some numbers will be divisible by more than one!)

Teacher Page

30

DIVIDE & CONQUER

To quickly determine if a number may be divided evenly by 2, 3, 4, 5, 6, 8, 9 or 10, simply remember these rules.

A number is divisible by 2 if the ones digit is even.

468 is divisible by 2 because 8 is even.

A number is divisible by 3 if the sum of its digits is divisible by 3.

3 + 7 + 5 = 15 15 is divisible by 3 — so 375 is, too!

A number is divisible by 4 if its last two digits are divisible by 4.

936 is divisible by 4 because 36 is divisible by 4!

A number is divisible by 5 if it ends in 0 or 5.

805, 500, 150, and 445

A number is divisible by 6 if it is divisible by both 2 and 3.

1674 is even (see rule for "divisible by 2"), and its digits add up to 18, which is divisible by 3.

A number is divisible by 8 if its last three digits are divisible by 8.

9360 is divisible by 8 because 360 is!

A number is divisible by 9 if the sum of its digits is divisible by 9.

95,769 is divisible by 9 because the sum of its digits equals 36, which is divisible by 9.

A number is divisible by 10 if its last digit is 0.

190, 2990, 70 and 650

Student Page

Name _____

TO CATCH A THIEF

Catch a thief by finding out exactly how much is in the bag. The clues will help you.

Clues:
6 bills under $50 each
  (not all the same)
no $10 bills
no $1 bills
4 coins — 2 the same
no nickels

Clues:
20 bills — all the same
3 coins — all the same

Clue:
256 coins — all the same

Clues:
23 bills — 10 of one kind
              13 of one kind
2 coins — not the same
              no quarters
              no nickels

WHOLE NUMBERS

Whole Numbers
Estimation

Name _____

ON THE ROAD

Meet the rock band "Six Big Feet."

This is their fall schedule.

SCHEDULE

Sept 10	Winnipeg
Sept 12	Philadelphia
Sept 13	Nashville
Sept 14	Miami
Sept 16	Kansas City
Sept 17	Albuquerque
Sept 18	Los Angeles
Sept 20	Salt Lake City
Sept 21	Boise
Sept 22	Seattle
Sept 24	San Francisco

Use the map on the next page to estimate the number of miles they will have traveled by the end of the tour!

U.S. MAP

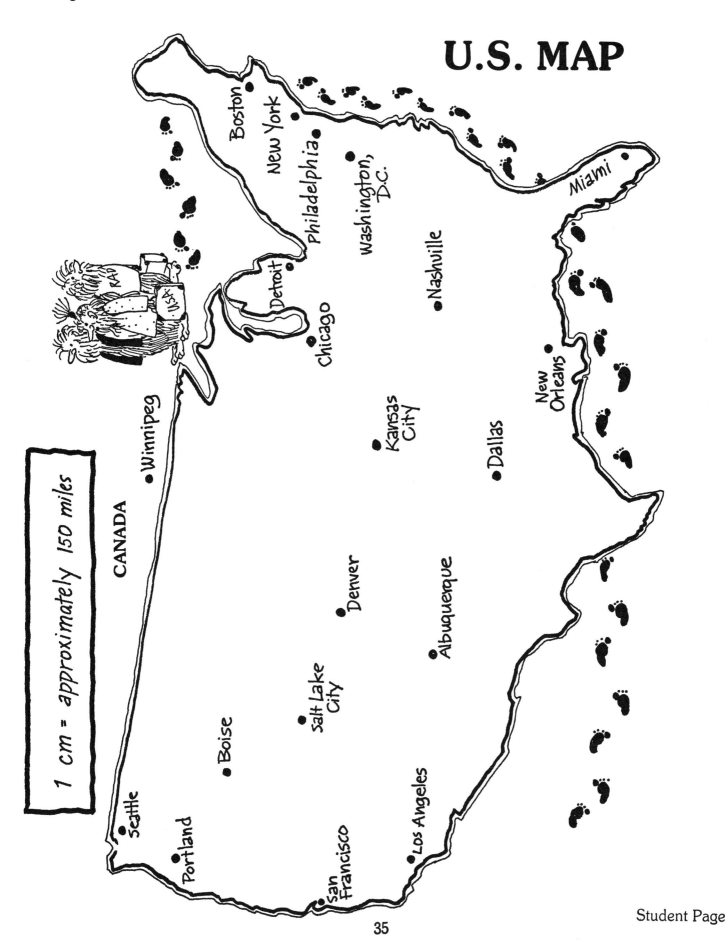

1 cm = approximately 150 miles

CANADA

Whole Numbers
Addition

TOO HOT TO HOOT

Take a number: 521
Reverse it: +125
Add: 646
Hooray!
   It's a palindrome!
Some take longer:
   814
  +418
  1232
 +2321
  3553
Take each answer and reverse it until you have a palindrome!

Preparation:
- Gather some ideas for palindromes — numbers, words, and phrases.

Use:
1) Ask students this question: "What does the number 7887 have in common with the words "level," "radar" and "too hot to hoot"?
   Let the class discover that all of the words read the same forward and backward. Such words are called palindromes.
2) Inform the students that addition produces palindromes. Demonstrate the procedure.
3) Have students use each number below to find a palindrome.

| 225 | 68 | 59 | 643 | 597 | 455 |
| 734 | 917 | 166,548 | 189 | 3516 | 89* |

* This one takes a lot of adding!

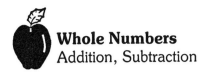

Whole Numbers
Addition, Subtraction

AN EAR FOR MATH

Preparation:
- Prepare a list of 15 questions similar to those below.

Use:
1) Substitute this "math by ear" activity for textbook or work sheet math one day. Ask students math problem questions such as these:

   What is 3902 increased by 587?
   How much greater is 9057 than 3889?
   How much less is 90,975 than 189,567?
   What is 5555 increased by 444?
   What is 743 minus 79?
   What number minus 26 plus 66 minus 25 is equal to 115?

2) Instruct students to listen to the questions, write the problems, and find the answers.

Teacher Page

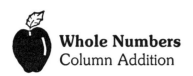

ASK THE CASH REGISTER

Preparation:
- Save enough receipts from cash registers for each student. (Students can help collect these.)

Use:
1) Cut the totals off of the cash register receipts.
2) Give each student one or more receipts. Ask the students "to be the cash registers" and find the missing totals.
3) For a more challenging task, leave the totals on the receipts and "white out" a few of the numbers in the columns. Have students find the missing numbers.

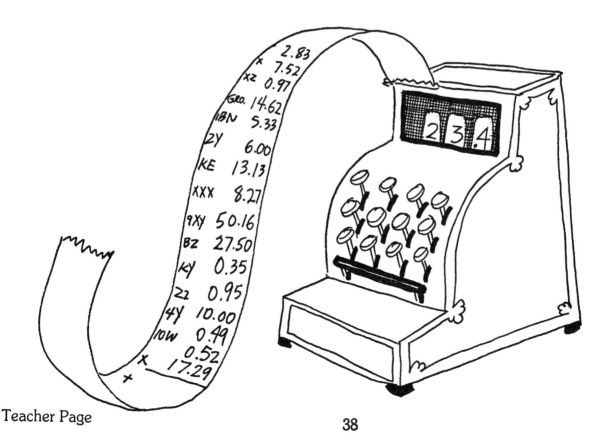

SUM SLALOM

Help Mogul Mouse break the
slalom record by adding the
column correctly.

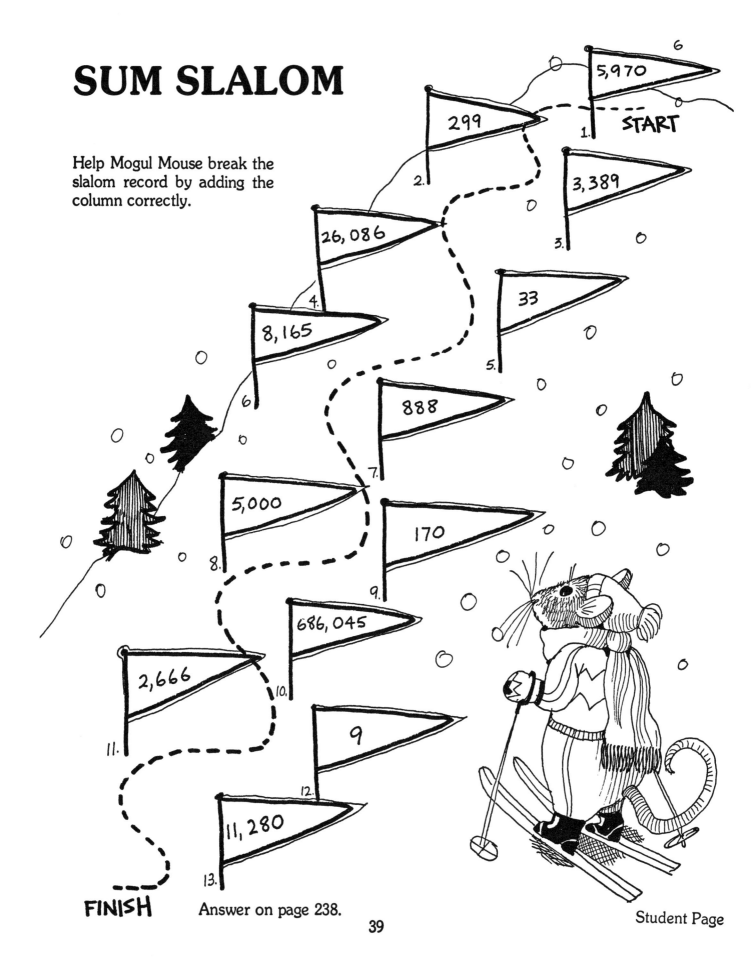

5,970   6

299   2.

START   1.

3,389   3.

26,086   4.

33   5.

8,165   6.

888   7.

5,000   8.

170   9.

686,045   10.

2,666   11.

9   12.

11,280   13.

FINISH

Answer on page 238.

39

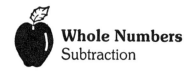
SPECTACULARLY STRANGE

Preparation:
- Make a strange shape or creature and write the number 6174 on it.

Use:
1) Tell students that there is something spectacularly strange about this particular number. Ask the students to help you make the number "appear."
2) Instruct the class to pick any four numbers from 0 to 9. Then proceed with the directions below.

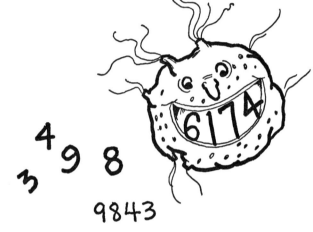

1. Arrange the four numbers to make the largest possible number.

$$9843$$

2. Arrange the four numbers to make the smallest possible number.
3. Subtract.
4. Take the answer and arrange the digits to make the largest possible number.

$$-3489$$
$$6354$$
$$6543$$

5. Arrange the digits in the answer to make the smallest possible number.

$$-3456$$
$$3087$$

6. Subtract.

$$8730$$
$$-378$$
$$8352$$

7. Repeat steps 4-7 with each answer until the chosen number appears.

$$8532$$
$$-2358$$
$$6174$$

Try this "spectacular" activity with other numbers!

Name _____

SKATEBOARD SUBTRACTION

Do the subtraction problems below to find out how many jellybeans the winner of the skateboard race will receive. Begin by subtracting 3,999 from 200,057,975. Then subtract the next number on the hill from that answer. Continue subtracting each number on the hill from the previous answer.

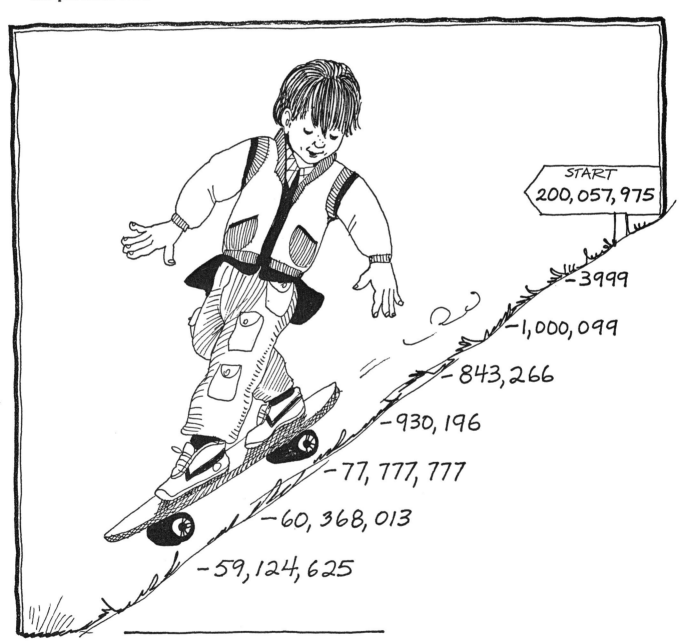

START
200,057,975

−3999

−1,000,099

−843,266

−930,196

−77,777,777

−60,368,013

−59,124,625

Answer on page 238.

Student Page

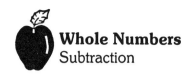

HOW TALL IS TALL?

Preparation:

- Have available a set of encyclopedias and other reference materials which may contain information about heights of buildings.
- Gather a supply of drawing paper, colored construction paper, rulers, scissors and markers.

Use:

1) Let students work in small groups to search in reference books for the names and heights of several of the world's tallest buildings. Students should pay special attention to any photographs or illustrations of the buildings.

2) Have each group or individual create a cut-out picture of one of the buildings. Instruct each group to determine a scale for their drawings so that the heights of the drawings are proportionate to the actual heights of the buildings.

3) Direct the groups to label their buildings with names and heights. Display the buildings on a wall or bulletin board.

4) Ask students to write five subtraction problems using the information on the buildings.

5) Students may trade problems so that each has five problems to solve.

Note: A <u>World Almanac</u> is a good source for this information.

Name _____

FASTER THAN A CHICKEN

TOP SPEEDS	
Animal	MPH
Cheetah	70
Antelope	61
Lion	50
Elk	45
Coyote	43
Zebra	40
Greyhound	40
Rabbit	35
Giraffe	32
Grizzly	30
Elephant	25
Black Mamba (snake)	20
Wild Turkey	15
Pig	11
Chicken	9
Spider	2

Let me at 'em! I can beat them! I can beat them all!

Use the chart above to answer the following questions.

1. What is the speed of a train that's three times as fast as a cheetah? _____

2. What animal is five times faster than a chicken? _____

3. Which animal is approximately three times faster than an elephant? _____

4. The pig is approximately five times as fast as what animal? _____

5. A _____ is twice as fast as a black mamba.

6. What animal is 35 times faster than a spider? _____

7. Which animal travels at three times the speed of a turkey? _____

8. Which animals are more than three times as fast as a pig, but not four times as fast?

    _____

9. How do the speeds of the grizzly and the antelope compare? _____

    _____

10. Which animal is almost twice as fast as a giraffe? _____

Answers on page 238.

Student Page

CATCH A FACTOR

Preparation:
- You will need light brown or orange construction paper, scissors, markers and tape.
- Make several poster board circles decorated to resemble baseballs, each with one of these numbers written on it.

50	18	1000	28	49	72
36	12	26	16	44	35
15	42	91	88	32	30
20	99	27	9	11	18
30	64	56	70	55	77

Use:
1) Review with students the concept of factoring. Work together to find the factors of several numbers not listed above.
2) Give each student a baseball and ask him or her to make a baseball glove on which to write the factors of the number on the ball.
3) Tape the baseball and glove shapes to walls, windows, and other objects around the room.
4) Use part of one math period for students to match each factor glove with the correct baseball. Students may write their answers on paper.

Whole Numbers
Prime Factorization

Name _____

FACTOR TREES

Any composite number can be written as a product of prime factors.

To find the prime factors, find any two factors. Then find the factors of these numbers. Continue factoring until you have only prime numbers.

A factor tree will help. The last row contains all prime factors.

Finish each factor tree and write the prime factors.

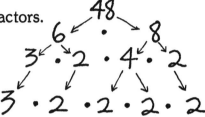

①.

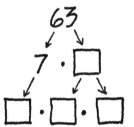

③.

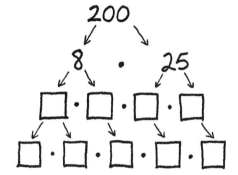

②.

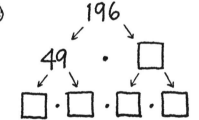

④.

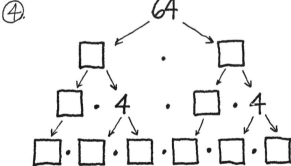

Use the back of this paper to make a factor tree for each of the following numbers.

⑤. 250 _____

⑥. 120 _____

⑦. 81 _____

⑧. 162 _____

Student Page

45

NAPIER'S BONES

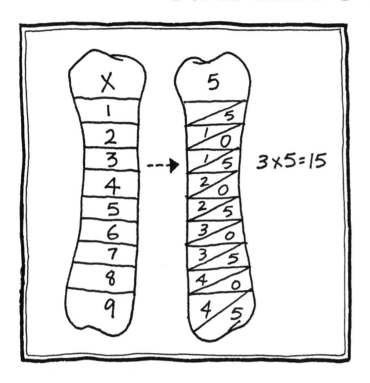

$3 \times 5 = 15$

Preparation:
- Provide each student with a pair of scissors and 10 tongue depressors or a piece of poster board.
- Make a copy of the student page "Napier's Bones" for each student.

Use:
1) Explain the history of Napier's bones to the class.

John Napier, a Scottish mathematician who lived about 400 years ago, invented a simple calculator which used rods to multiply any number by a one-digit number. These rods are called Napier's bones because the rods were sometimes made of bone.

2) Show students how to use Napier's bones. Solve a few multiplication and division problems together. Then, ask the students to solve the problems on the student page.

To multiply 3 x 5, find the section on the 3 bone which corresponds to the 5 on the index bone. The number in this section is the answer.

To multiply more than one digit (847 x 3), multiply one digit at a time and then add as shown.

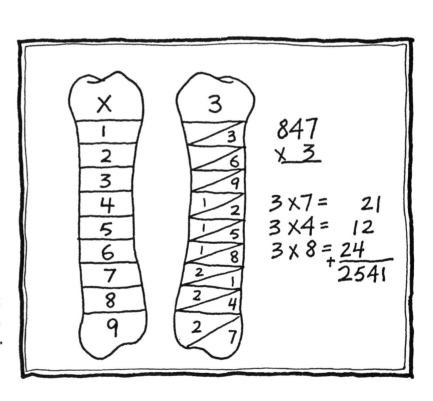

$$847 \\ \times\ 3$$

$$3 \times 7 = \quad 21$$
$$3 \times 4 = \quad 12$$
$$3 \times 8 = \underline{+\ 24}$$
$$ 2541$$

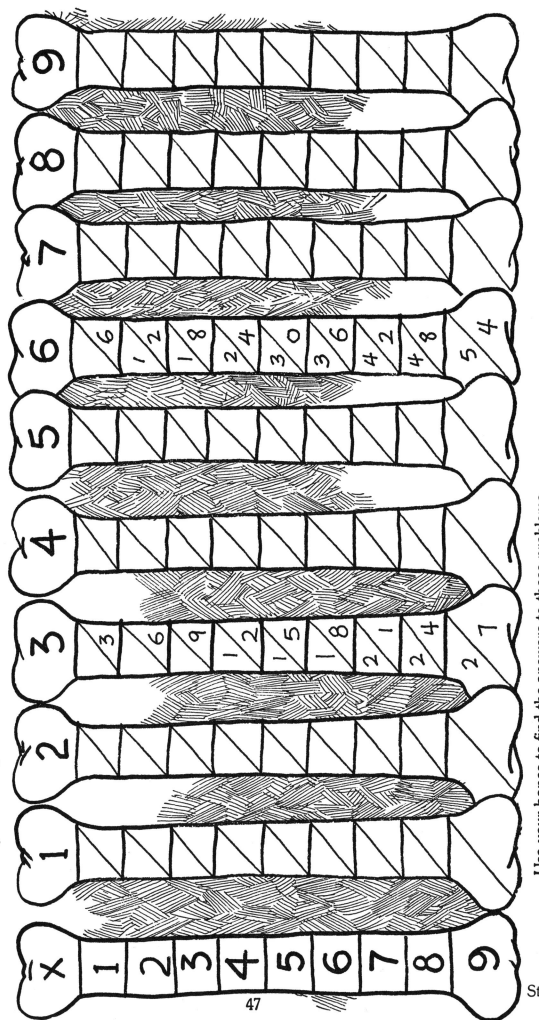

NAPIER'S BONES

Whole Numbers
Multiplication

Name _____

Complete the bones by filling in the remaining products. (See examples.) Then glue each bone on a tongue depressor or cardboard strip.

Now you're ready to use one of the world's first calculators!

Use your bones to find the answers to these problems.

a. 845 x 7   b. 635 x 9   c. 9064 x 4   d. 3456 x 5

e. 964 x 6   f. 3860 x 9   g. 947 x 8   h. 6686 x 3

Student Page

47

Whole Numbers
Division

FIND THE MISTRAKES

Preparation:
- Gather white construction paper or poster board, scissors, and black markers.
- If possible, make a large drawing of a sleuth, detective, spy, or another such character who would search for "clues."

Use:
1) Have each student make a large magnifying glass shape.
2) Instruct each student to write a division problem with an incorrect answer on the magnifying glass. There must be only one mistake.
3) Number the magnifying glasses and post them around the room. Require each student to choose 10 of the problems, identify each mistake, and then solve the problems correctly.

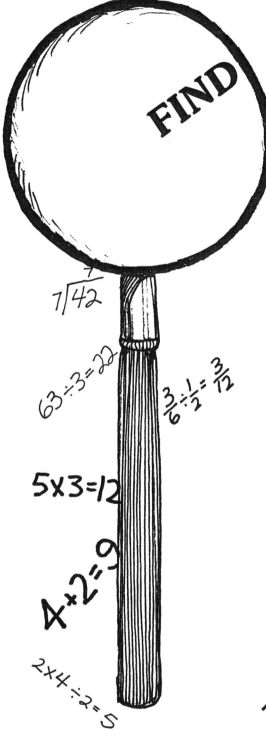

$7\overline{)42}$ with 7 on top

$63 \div 3 = 22$

$\frac{3}{6} \div \frac{1}{2} = \frac{3}{12}$

$5 \times 3 = 12$

$4 \div 2 = 9$

$2 \times 4 \div 2 = 5$

$27 \div 3 = 6$

$45 + 18 = 53$

JUMPING THE HURDLES

Help Helen Hurdler over the hurdles and find out what the amount of the prize money is.

Begin with the number shown at START. When you come to the first hurdle, divide by the divisor shown there.

Divide the answer by the divisor shown on the second hurdle, and so on.

START:

$ 734,580,000.00

÷ BY 80

÷ BY 3

÷ BY 265

÷ BY 21

÷ BY 22

PRIZE IS:

$ _____

Answer on page 238.

49

Student Page

TIME OUT FOR BUBBLES

BUBBLES

½ cup liquid
   detergent
2 cups water
2 Tbs. Salad oil
   Mix gently!
BLOW with straws or
bent wire loops.

Preparation:
- Gather six mixing bowls, six spoons, lots of straws, some thin wire, scissors, a large bottle of liquid detergent, and a bottle of salad oil.

Use:
- Practice finding averages by blowing and counting homemade bubbles. Here's how:
1) Divide the class into five or six groups. Each group makes a batch of bubble suds by following the recipe above.
2) Allow students to take turns blowing bubbles. Group members must count and record the number of bubbles produced by each blow.
3) When every group member has had a turn blowing bubbles, the group should calculate the average number of bubbles per blow.

Teacher Page

THE AVERAGE CLASSROOM

Preparation:

- Compile a list of ideas for averages which would "apply" to your classroom and/or students. (See the examples below.)

Use:

1) Dedicate one math period to the exploration of your "average" classroom. Write your compiled list of ideas for averages on the board. Tell students that the class is to find the averages for the items on the board. They will need to decide on a procedure for doing this. One pair of students might take responsibility for each item, etc.

Average daily class attendance for one week

Average height of students in inches

Average shoe size

Average number of siblings

Average number of students buying lunch each day for one week

Average weight of textbooks

Average distance between eyes

Average length of tongue

Average student age in years and months

Average circumference of head

Average number of teeth

HOLD IT! THE GLARE'S GETTING TO ME!

Teacher Page

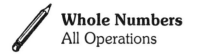

Name _____

WHICH TREASURE TO DIG?

These kids are on a treasure hunt with only this map to help them find the right spot to dig. Every time they come to a division in the road, they must solve a problem and go in the direction shown by the right answer.

Can you figure out which treasure they will dig? Trace the correct route with a pencil.

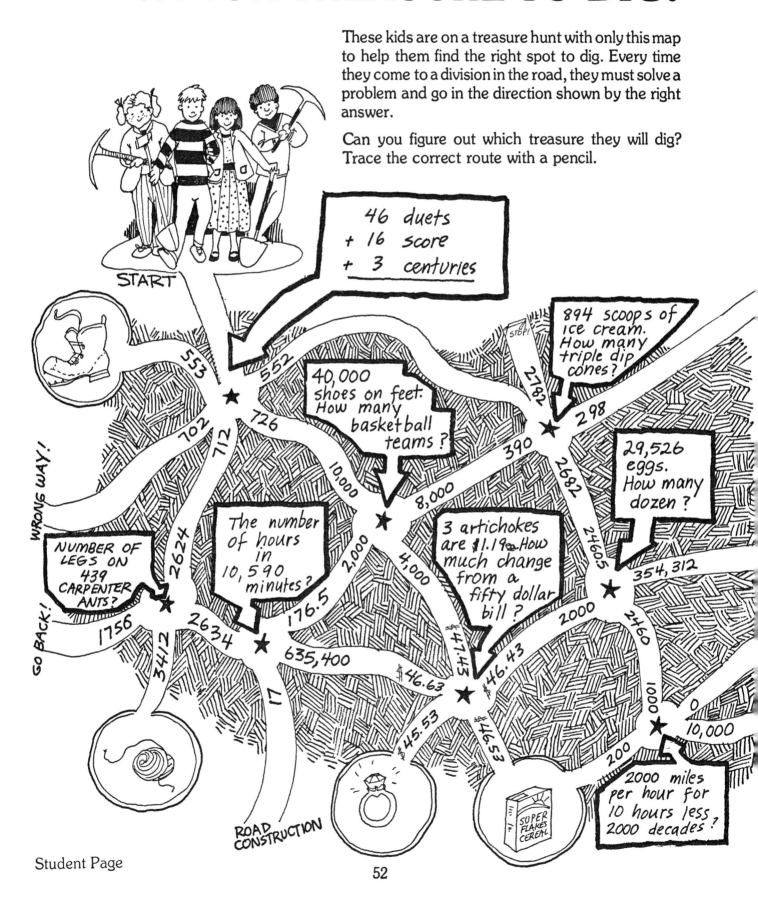

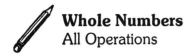

Whole Numbers
All Operations

Name _____

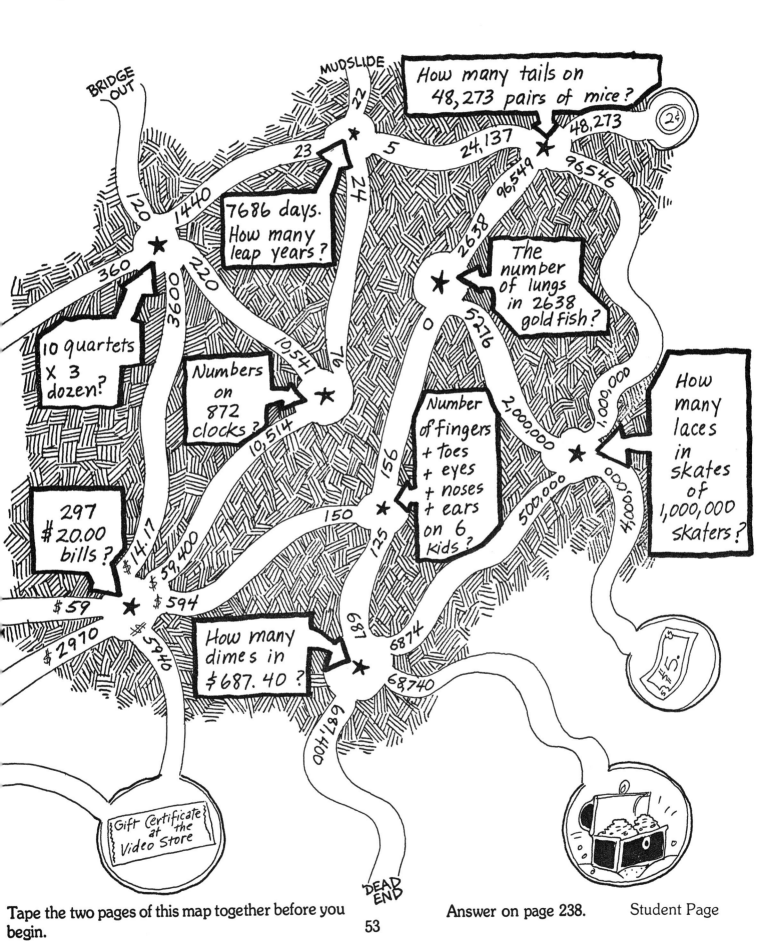

Tape the two pages of this map together before you begin.

Answer on page 238.   Student Page

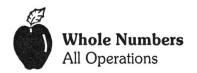

VERY PERSONAL

Preparation:
- Write ideas for personal numbers on the board. (See the examples below.)

Use:
1) Ask students to think of "personal numbers" such as:

   birth dates (Example: 10-30 for October 30)
   ages
   addresses
   social security numbers
   amounts of money in piggy banks
   etc.

2) Have the class add to the list of ideas on the board. Instruct each student to make a record of individual personal numbers on a sheet of paper.

3) Ask each student to write and solve 10 math problems using their list of numbers, making use of all four math operations. Or have students write 10 math problems, trade papers, and solve problems created by classmates.

Name _____

SURPRISE!

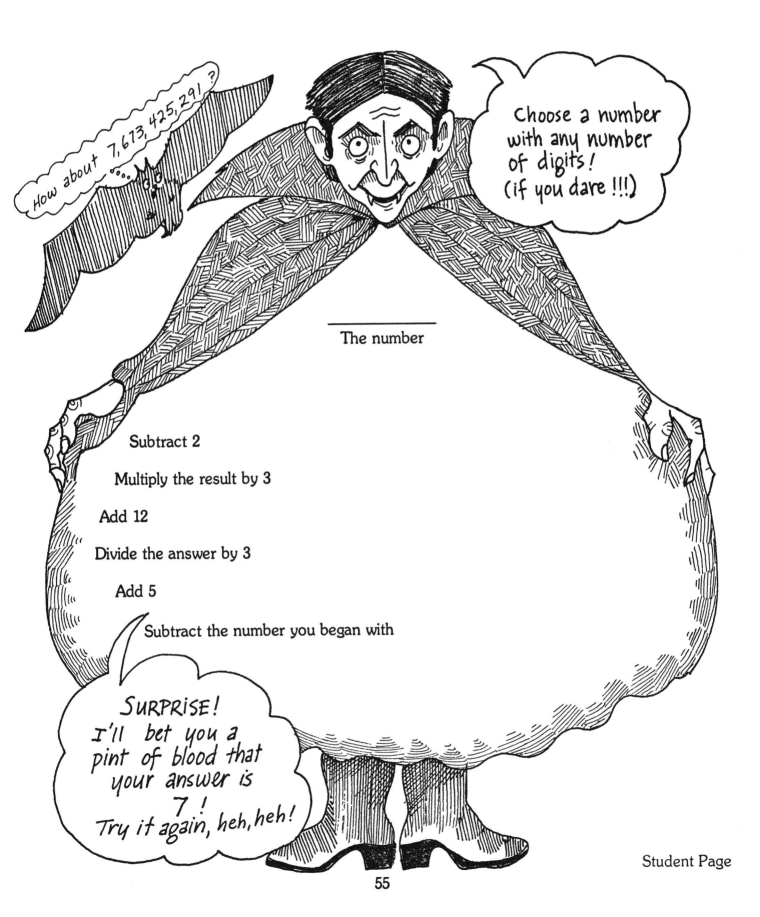

The number _____

Subtract 2

Multiply the result by 3

Add 12

Divide the answer by 3

Add 5

Subtract the number you began with

Name _____

WANTED!

Each culprit is hiding under an assumed number name. Catch them all by using the clue to find each number!

1. Dangerous Dorothy

toes on a quartet times days in April

2. Slim Chance

79 dozen minus 948

3. Divisive Dan

legs on 327 flies

4. Samantha Sneaker

total shoes in 1,000,687 pairs

5. Bad, Bad Barb

bicentennial year of the Declaration of Independence minus your ears

6. Muscles McGroo

inches in 5 yards minus minutes in 3/4 hour

Name _____

7. Jumpy Jake

16 centuries
divided by 8 decades

8. snakebite Sally

this year minus
months in a year

9. Louise Lightfingers

minutes in $27\frac{1}{3}$ hours

10. Pete Pickpocket

elbows on 46 mosquitoes

11. Snatchin' Sam

lines in a limerick times
legs on a football team

12. Elusive Ellie

pints in 82 gallons

57

Student Page

PUZZLE MAKERS

Preparation:
- You will need a supply of white drawing paper and rulers.
- Duplicate enough copies of the student page "Cross Numbers" for all of your students.

Use:
1) Have students work to complete the cross number puzzle on the student page.
2) When all students have finished, ask them to pay special attention to the way the puzzle is made.
3) Provide time for students to create their own puzzles. Suggest that they follow this procedure:
    - Make the puzzle shape first, putting any numbers into spaces. (The shape, size, and layout may be different from the sample.)
    - Place letters at appropriate spots for "across" and "down" columns.
    - Create a math problem which will serve as a clue for each number in the puzzle.
4) Students may trade and solve finished puzzles.

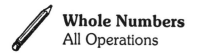

Whole Numbers
All Operations

Name _____

CROSS NUMBERS

Work the problems to solve this puzzle.
Show your calculations on a separate piece of
paper.

ACROSS
A   49 x 107
B   25 x 107
D   25,640 − 16,373
F   (72 x 106) + 1770
G   8 x 507
I   55,476 ÷ 69

DOWN
A   4048 ÷ 8
B   (850 ÷ 50) + 10
C   (15,000 ÷ 30) + 34
E   60 x 70
H   1,000,000 ÷ 20

Answers on pages 238.

59

Student Page

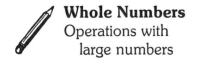

Name _____

GETTING AROUND THE SOLAR SYSTEM

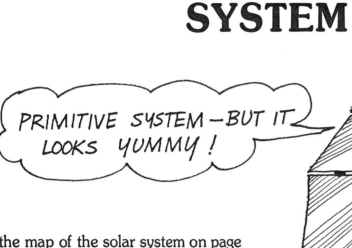

PRIMITIVE SYSTEM — BUT IT LOOKS YUMMY !

Use the map of the solar system on page 61 to help these space travelers answer some questions about the solar system.

1) If the space travelers are planning to travel from Jupiter to Saturn, how much farther would it be to go to Pluto?

2) When Uranus has orbited the sun once, how much longer will it take Neptune to get around the sun?

3) What planet is about four times farther from the sun than Mercury?

4) What distance will the space travelers cover between Mars and Uranus?

5) How much closer to the sun is Venus than Neptune?

6) What planet's orbit takes approximately six times as long as Mars' orbit?

7) Approximately how many more days than Jupiter does Pluto take to orbit the sun?

8) What orbit takes approximately 2600 times as long as that of Venus?

Name _____

SOLAR SYSTEM MAP

Whole Numbers
Operations with
large numbers

Distances From Sun		Time To Orbit Sun
Mercury	36,000,000	88 days
Venus	67,000,000	225 days
Earth	93,000,000	1 year
Mars	142,000,000	687 days
Jupiter	484,000,000	12 years
Saturn	885,000,000	29.5 years
Uranus	1,780,000,000	84 years
Neptune	2,790,000,000	164 years
Pluto	3,660,000,000	247 years

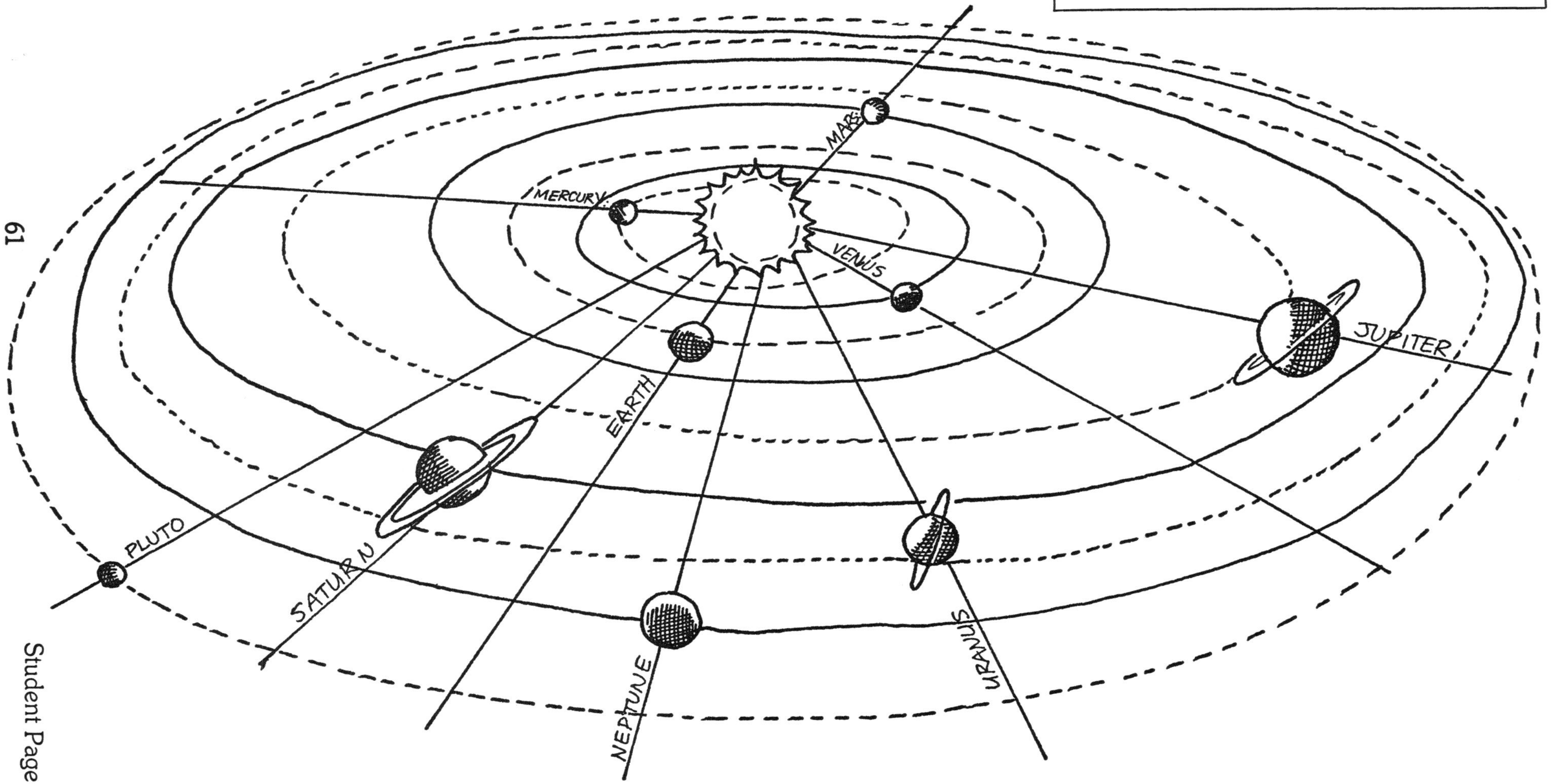

Student Page

Name _____

YOUR WISH IS MY COMMAND

1. 4730

2. 100,365,198

3. 29,689

4. 27,298

5. 60,539,007

6. 10,001

7. 2,983,400

8. 886,345

9. 29

10. 4

11. 800,444

12. 123,456,789

100 TIMES GREATER

10,000 TIMES GREATER

1000 TIMES GREATER

This genie magically makes everything 100 times greater. What will each of these numbers become?

This genie has already made each number 10,000 times greater. What was each original number?

This genie makes everything 1000 times greater. What will these numbers be?

Student Page

62

Answers on page 238.

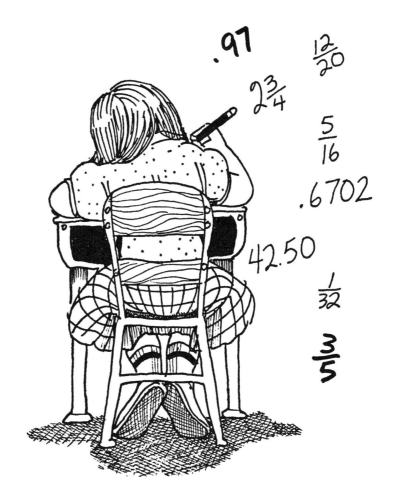

.97 $\frac{12}{20}$

$2\frac{3}{4}$

$\frac{5}{16}$

.6702

42.50 $\frac{1}{32}$

$\frac{3}{5}$

FRACTIONS & DECIMALS

A FRACTION HUNT

Preparation:

- Prepare a list of questions that will help students locate fractions in the classroom. (See the ideas below.)

Use:

1) Fractions are everywhere! Have students search for and identify fractions in the classroom.

2) To help students name parts of sets with fractions, ask them questions such as those below.

What fraction tells:

> how many of the people in this class are boys? Girls?
> how many students are new to the school this year?
> how many in this class are wearing black shoes?
> how many in this class have curly hair?
> how many of the pencils in the room are dull?
> how many of the desks have writing on them?

3) After the students have practiced writing "classroom fractions," give each student a copy of the student page "A Fraction Around Every Corner" and allow time for "fraction hunting." When everyone has finished, let them compare answers.

Teacher Page

Name _____

A FRACTION AROUND EVERY CORNER

Did you hear that $\frac{4}{5}$ of the students ate the school lunch yesterday........?

...Yes, And $\frac{4}{5}$ went home sick!

Write fractions for the following items.

people in your school that are teachers _____

teachers in your school that are female _____ male _____

the part of the day taken up by lunch period _____

classrooms that have a sink _____

students that are 6th graders _____

females in your grade _____

students that have had perfect attendance all year _____

rooms that are not "classrooms" _____

students who ate the school lunch today _____

Find at least two more fractions relating to your school and write them here:

65

Student Page

OUT OF ORDER

Preparation:
- Make six sets of large cards (15 x 15 cm). Write one of the fractions below on each card.

Use:
1) Review with students the method for comparing fractions and determining which is larger or smaller.

Cross multiply to determine whether $\frac{9}{10}$ is larger than $\frac{1}{4}$.

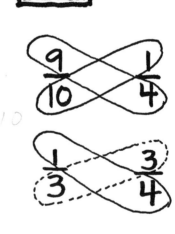

Since the product of 9 x 4 is larger than that of 10 x 1, the first fraction is larger.

Which is larger, $\frac{1}{3}$ or $\frac{3}{4}$?

Since the product of 1 x 4 is less than 3 x 3, the first fraction is smaller.

2) Practice comparing fractions as a class. When students feel comfortable with the procedure, give each student a copy of the student page "Order's Up!" to complete.

Teacher Page

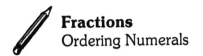

Name _____

ORDER'S UP!

This is what Julia ordered for lunch at the Fractionville Diner.

At the Fractionville Diner, food items are served to you in the order of the size of the fraction on each food — beginning with the smallest fraction. Draw each food item in the space below in the order they will be served to Julia.

Fractions
Addition
Subtraction

PIZZA PROBLEMS

Preparation:
- Gather a collection of pizza-sized cardboard circles, colored construction paper, markers, scissors, and glue.

Use:
1) Brainstorm a list of all of the possible toppings for pizza.
2) Allow plenty of time for each student to construct a pizza using a cardboard circle for the crust and using various art materials to make "homemade" toppings.
3) When the pizzas are complete, students should "cut" them by using a wide-tipped marker to divide them evenly into 4,5,6,7,8,9 or more slices.
4) Display the pizzas at the front of the room where they can be easily seen.
5) Students may use the different-sized slices to make addition and subtraction pizza problems. Have each student write 10 problems and then trade with a classmate who will solve them.

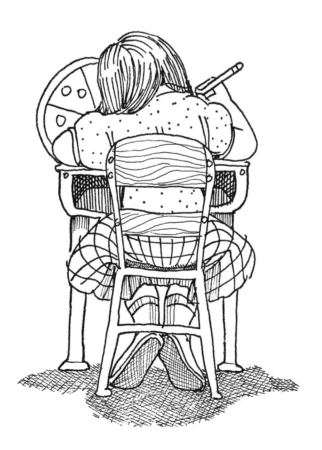

Teacher Page

68

Name _____

HOW LOW CAN YOU GO?

Only fractions in lowest terms can pass under this bar.

Circle the people below that will make it under the bar.

Write any fractions that are not in lowest terms in the box at the bottom of the page. Then reduce each fraction to lowest terms.

A MATTER OF EQUIVALENCY

Preparation:

- "Hide" the fractions below in locations around the room where they may be found without too much difficulty.

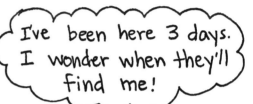

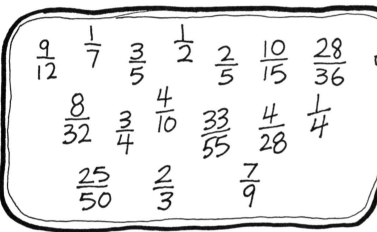

$$\frac{9}{12} \quad \frac{1}{7} \quad \frac{3}{5} \quad \frac{1}{2} \quad \frac{2}{5} \quad \frac{10}{15} \quad \frac{28}{36}$$

$$\frac{8}{32} \quad \frac{3}{4} \quad \frac{4}{10} \quad \frac{33}{55} \quad \frac{4}{28} \quad \frac{1}{4}$$

$$\frac{25}{50} \quad \frac{2}{3} \quad \frac{7}{9}$$

Use:

1) Review with students the definition of equivalent fractions and the cross-multiplication method for determining whether two fractions are equivalent.

$$\frac{2}{5} \text{ is equivalent to } \frac{8}{20}$$

$$2 \times 20 = 5 \times 8$$

2) Inform the students that there are eight pairs of equivalent fractions "lurking" around the room. Students should find the fractions and try to match the pairs properly.

3) Follow this lesson with the activity found on the student page "Find The Impostor."

Fractions
Equivalents

Name _____

FIND THE IMPOSTOR

Each of these fractions is pretending to be equivalent to all of the others. All of them are equivalent except for one.

Find the impostor.

A GHOSTLY BRUNCH

Preparation:
- Make copies of the following student page "Ghoulash In A Flash" for your students.

Use:
1) Work as a class to adjust the "ghoulash" recipe ingredient amounts to make only $\frac{2}{3}$ of the "ghoulash."
2) Brainstorm other ideas of unusual "brews" and recipes such as those below.

Vampire cheese bites	Toasted "ghostwitches"
Dracula dip	Cemetery stew
Cat's eye soufflé	Buttered bat bread

3) Allow time for each student to create an original recipe. Instruct them to write the recipes clearly and to attach an instruction for changing the amount made. (i.e. Make $2\frac{1}{2}$ batches; prepare $\frac{3}{4}$ of the recipe; make enough for 25 ghosts, etc.)
4) Have students trade recipes and follow the instructions to alter the recipes.

Name _____

GHOULASH IN A FLASH

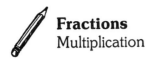

GHOULASH

3½ pounds	MOTH DUST	1	IGUANA TOOTH
2⅔ quarts	GOBLIN GREASE	4⅞ quarts	RAT BLOOD
¼ cup	LIZARD SCALES	1⅔	BAT WINGS
1⅖ cups	TOAD WARTS	½	VAMPIRE TONGUE
5⅓ gallons	SPIDER BROTH	2¾ cups	MASHED MONSTER MEAT

Directions: Fry monster meat for one hour. Add goblin grease, spider broth, rat blood and bat wings and simmer two days. Chop lizard scales, iguana tooth, and vampire tongue and stir into mixture. Sprinkle the top with moth dust.

Serves: 36 hungry ghouls

Twenty-four ghouls are coming to your midnight mania party. You'll need to prepare only 2/3 of the ghoulash recipe. Adjust the ingredients in the blanks below.

_____ moth dust

_____ goblin grease

_____ lizard scales

_____ toad warts

_____ spider broth

_____ iguana tooth

_____ rat blood

_____ vampire tongue

_____ bat wings

_____ mashed monster meat

IS IT DINNER YET?

Answers on page 239.

Student Page

WHAT'S COOKING?

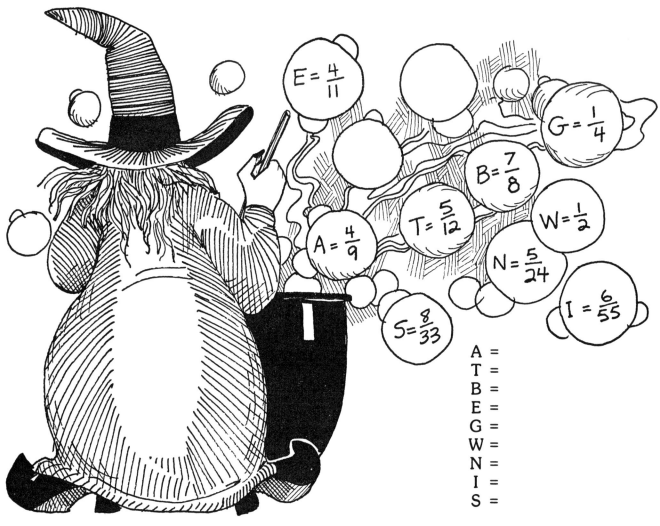

A =
T =
B =
E =
G =
W =
N =
I =
S =

In the bubbling brew there is a correct answer for each problem. To find out what the witch is cooking, solve each problem, beginning with the top left corner, and write the letter of the correct answer in the corresponding blank below.

$$\frac{3}{2} \div \frac{12}{7} \qquad \frac{4}{5} \div \frac{9}{5} \qquad \frac{4}{9} \div \frac{16}{15} \qquad \frac{3}{4} \div \frac{3}{2} \qquad \frac{6}{10} \div \frac{11}{2} \qquad \frac{6}{12} \div \frac{12}{5} \qquad \frac{9}{18} \div \frac{2}{1}$$

$$\frac{8}{11} \div \frac{6}{2} \qquad \frac{2}{3} \div \frac{16}{10} \qquad \frac{2}{11} \div \frac{5}{10} \qquad \frac{7}{10} \div \frac{7}{5}$$

___ ___ ___ ___ ___ ___ ___

___ ___ ___ ___

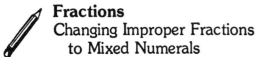

Fractions
Changing Improper Fractions
to Mixed Numerals

Name _____

HOW IMPROPER!

Find all of the improper fractions hiding in the picture.
Change each one to a mixed numeral in lowest terms.

Student Page

WHICH DOCTOR . . . .

These doctors are surgeons, but each one does only one kind of "operation": addition, subtraction, multiplication, or division. (See their labels.) Actually, each surgeon needs a little help with his or her "operation."

Notice the chart that gives the name of the doctor treating each pair of patients in pictures A through F. Help complete the surgery by performing the correct operation on each pair of patients.

Dr. Ida Payne   Dr. So. U. Up   Dr. Needles   Dr. U. R. Well
    +   —   ×   ÷

A. Dr. Ida Payne $5\frac{1}{2}$ $\frac{9}{10}$

B. Dr. U.R. Well $\frac{2}{9}$ $\frac{6}{11}$

Name _____

...DOES THE DOCTORING?

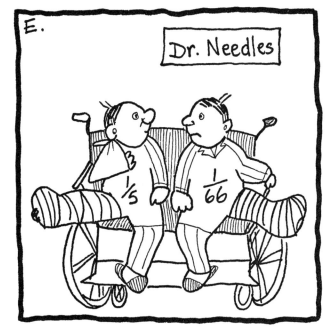

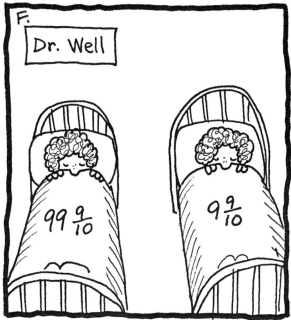

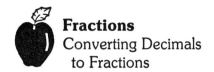

Fractions
Converting Decimals
to Fractions

NO DECIMALS ALLOWED

Preparation:

- Label as many classroom items as you can with related decimal numerals. For instance:

the height of a chair	weight of a book
dimensions of a calendar	cost of a map
temperature of the room	capacity of a lunch box

Use:

1) Ask students to find at least 15 objects labeled with decimals in the room.
2) For each object, the student should write the decimal on paper and then rewrite it as a fraction or mixed fraction number in lowest terms.

Name _____

THE ROVING DECIMAL

Where does the decimal belong?
Read each numeral and then put the decimal point in the right spot.

2 0 6 9 3 4	two thousand sixty-nine and thirty-four hundredths
8 7 8 2	eight hundred seventy-eight and two tenths
0 5 3 7	five hundred thirty-seven thousandths
1 0 6 6 2	ten and six hundred sixty-two thousandths

Draw a line to match each numeral with its correct description.

one thousand forty-three and seven tenths	1 0 4 . 3 7
one hundred four and thirty-seven hundredths	1 . 0 4 3 7
ten and four hundred thirty-seven thousandths	1 0 4 3 . 7
one and four hundred thirty-seven ten thousandths	1 0 . 4 3 7

Student Page

79

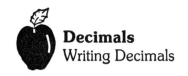
DECIMALS BY EAR

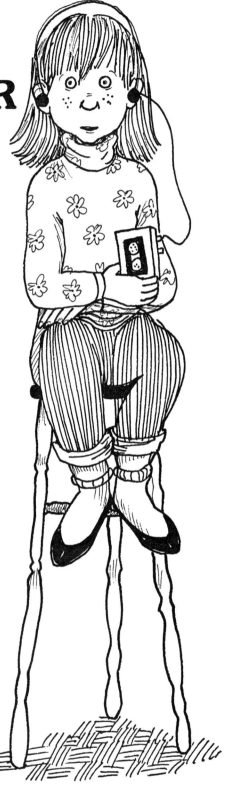

Preparation:

- On a cassette tape, record yourself saying several decimal numerals. For instance:

    a) three hundred and four
       thousandths
    b) nine and sixty-five hundredths
    c) seven hundred twenty thousandths

- Have a cassette player available for student use.

Use:

1) Give students individual or group practice at writing decimal numerals by letting them listen to dictation.
2) Students may listen to each numeral and then write the numeral on paper.
3) For easy correction, dictate the answers at the end of the tape or ask the student to give the paper and the tape to another student to check.

Name _____

STAR TREKS

Follow the directions beneath each spacecraft to round every number in its lane.

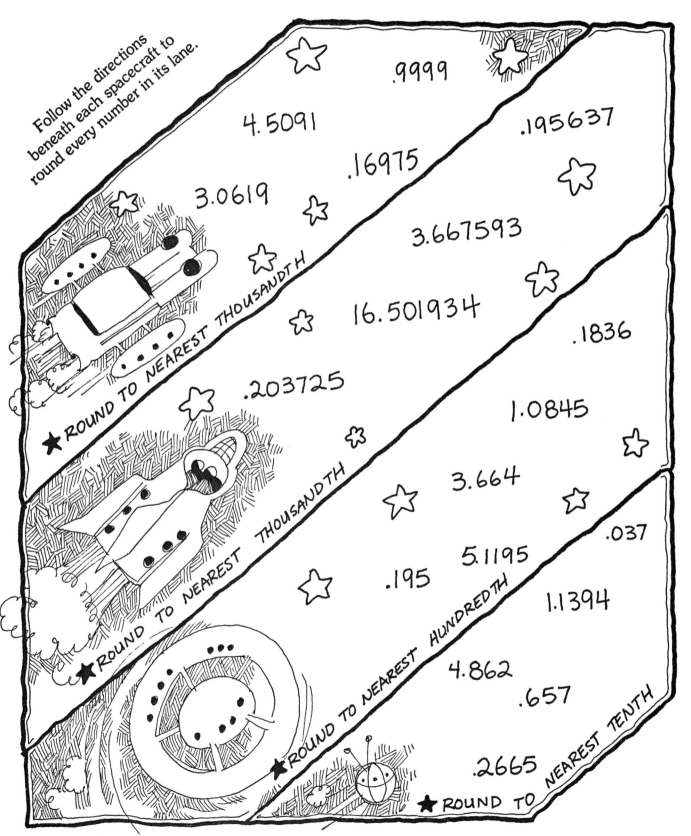

.9999

4.5091

.195637

.16975

3.0619

3.667593

★ ROUND TO NEAREST THOUSANDTH

16.501934

.1836

.203725

1.0845

★ ROUND TO NEAREST THOUSANDTH

3.664

.037

.195

5.1195

1.1394

★ ROUND TO NEAREST HUNDREDTH

4.862

.657

.2665

★ ROUND TO NEAREST TENTH

Student Page

GIVE ME A HAND

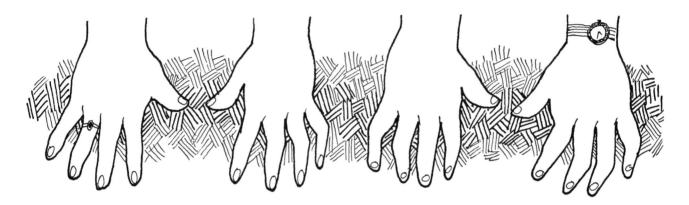

Preparation:
- Have metric rulers, meter sticks, string, and scissors available.

Use:
1) Talk with students about the use of a hand span to measure things (such as the height of a horse).
2) Practice measuring things by hand spans.

   heights of people   the doorway
   desk tops   wastebasket circumference

3) Talk about how one could translate such a measurement into meters and centimeters. Have each student measure his or her own hand span to find a measurement to the nearest tenth of a centimeter.
4) Allow students to compare hand span measurements with one another.
5) Give each student a copy of the student page "What Big Hands You Have!" and allow time for completing the tasks.

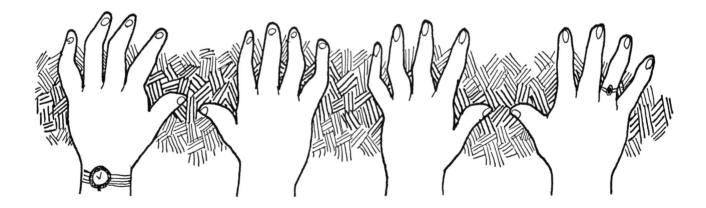

Decimals
Writing Measurements
Multiplication

Name _____

WHAT BIG HANDS YOU HAVE!

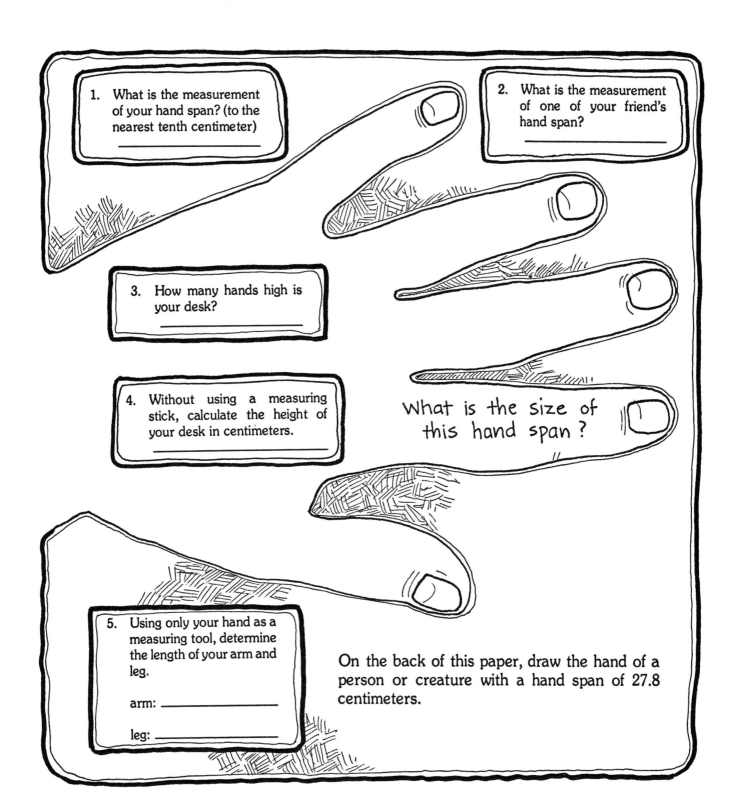

1. What is the measurement of your hand span? (to the nearest tenth centimeter)

   _____

2. What is the measurement of one of your friend's hand span?

   _____

3. How many hands high is your desk?

   _____

4. Without using a measuring stick, calculate the height of your desk in centimeters.

   _____

What is the size of this hand span?

5. Using only your hand as a measuring tool, determine the length of your arm and leg.

   arm: _____

   leg: _____

On the back of this paper, draw the hand of a person or creature with a hand span of 27.8 centimeters.

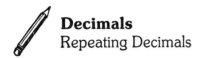

DECIMALS THAT REPEAT THEMSELVES

$$6\overline{)5.000000} = 0.8\overline{3}$$
.833333

When you divide 5 by 6, the quotient is a repeating decimal — a decimal which repeats the same digits, never having zero as a remainder. The line over the 3 in this example is a way of showing that the digit (or sometimes digits) repeats.

Work the problems below. Write each quotient as a repeating decimal.

a) $15\overline{)4}$ b) $6\overline{)1}$ c) $22\overline{)3}$ d) $12\overline{)1}$ e) $9\overline{)2}$

f) $3\overline{)2}$ g) $27\overline{)11}$ h) $3\overline{)1}$ i) $33\overline{)5}$ j) $37\overline{)8}$

Name _____

OLYMPIC CALCULATIONS

Here are the scores of the five gymnastic finalists. Find the average score for each girl.

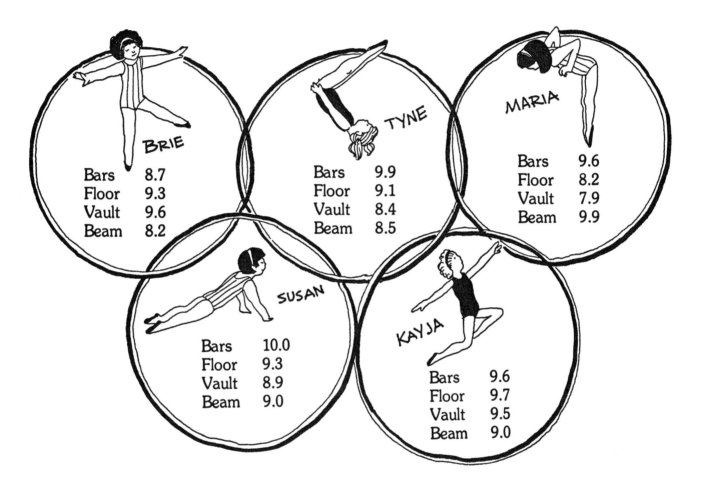

BRIE

Bars	8.7
Floor	9.3
Vault	9.6
Beam	8.2

TYNE

Bars	9.9
Floor	9.1
Vault	8.4
Beam	8.5

MARIA

Bars	9.6
Floor	8.2
Vault	7.9
Beam	9.9

SUSAN

Bars	10.0
Floor	9.3
Vault	8.9
Beam	9.0

KAYJA

Bars	9.6
Floor	9.7
Vault	9.5
Beam	9.0

		Name	Average Score
Who won the gold medal?	(first place)	_____	_____
Who won the silver medal?	(second)	_____	_____
Who won the bronze medal?	(third)	_____	_____

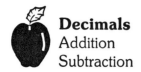

OUT OF POCKET EXPENSES

Preparation:
- Make copies of the student page "Who's The Big Spender?" for your students.

USE:
1) Review the process of adding and subtracting decimals.
2) Hand out copies of the student page. Discuss some ideas for creating word problems using the information on the page.
3) Create and solve a few problems as a class.
4) Tell students that they are to solve the problems on the student page to find out who is the biggest spender. Then students should write eight word problems using the information found in the picture. Each problem should include addition and/or subtraction.
5) Problems may be written on separate paper so that students may trade problems and solve those created by a classmate.

Teacher Page

Name _____

WHO'S THE BIG SPENDER?

Which person has spent the most money?

_____

_____

How much more did he or she spend than
the one who spent the least? _____

Use the information here to make up your own
problems using decimals.

87

Name _____

WATCH OUT FOR THE TEETH

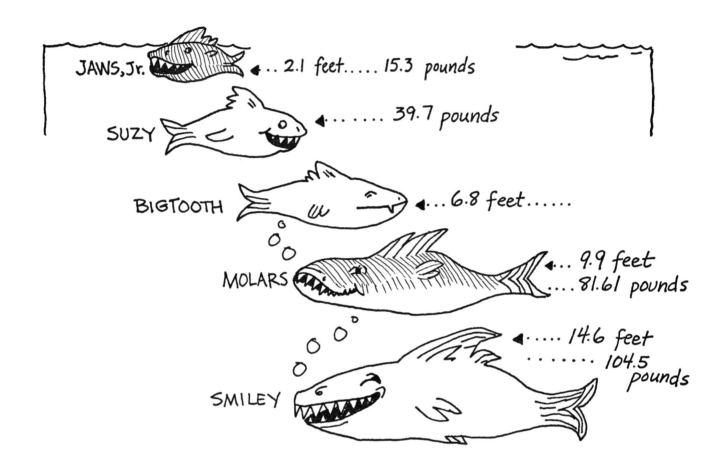

JAWS, Jr. ◄... 2.1 feet..... 15.3 pounds

SUZY ◄....... 39.7 pounds

BIGTOOTH ◄... 6.8 feet......

MOLARS ◄... 9.9 feet
....81.61 pounds

SMILEY ◄..... 14.6 feet
.... 104.5 pounds

1) Who is about 3.2 times the length of Jaws, Jr.? _____

2) Molars will increase her weight 0.35 times in the next year. What will she weigh then?

3) Bigtooth weighs about 0.61 as much as Smiley. How much does Bigtooth weigh? ____

4) Suzy is 0.37 the length of Smiley. How long is Suzy? _____

5) If an average shark eats 0.42 times its weight a day, about how much will each shark eat?

Suzy _____ Bigtooth _____ Molars _____

Smiley _____ Jaws, Jr. _____

Decimals
Division

WORKING IT OUT

Preparation:
- You will need large drawing paper or poster board, markers and crayons, black construction paper and scissors.
- Gather pictures of weight lifters and/or make copies of this page.

Use:
1) Have the class make 10 to 15 weight lifters using the provided art materials. Students may work in pairs or small groups.
2) Students should make a barbell for each weight lifter. Have the students write two decimals on each barbell.
3) Number the weight lifters and display them around the room as if they are lifting the barbells.
4) Ask students to write and solve a division problem for each pair of decimals. (Right hand number serving as the divisor.) Instruct students to find the largest quotient in order to determine which weight lifter has lifted the most weight.

 **Decimals**
Division

Name _____

OUT OF GAS

All of the vehicles below are out of gas. You can see how many miles each has traveled. Each vehicle had a full tank of gas when it started. The size of the tank is shown for each. For every vehicle, tell how many miles it traveled per gallon of gas.

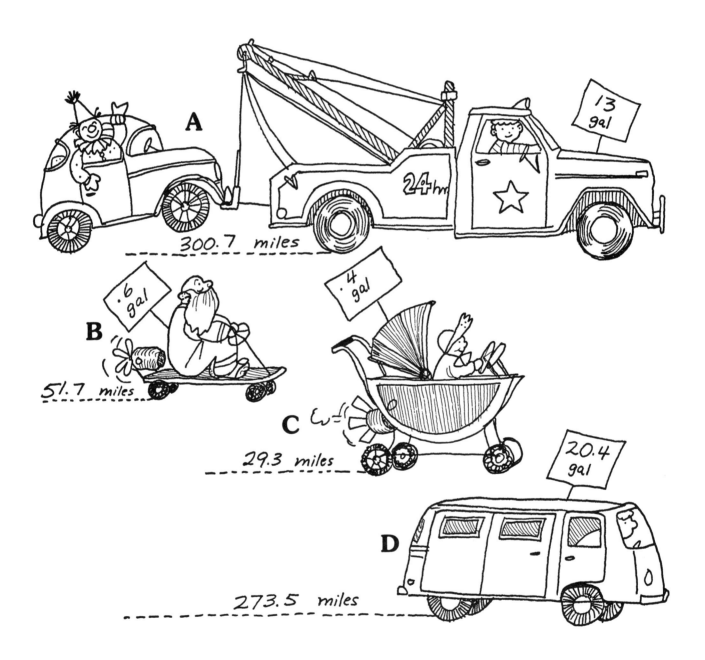

A

13 gal

300.7 miles

B

.6 gal

51.7 miles

C

.4 gal

29.3 miles

D

20.4 gal

273.5 miles

Decimals
Division

Name _____

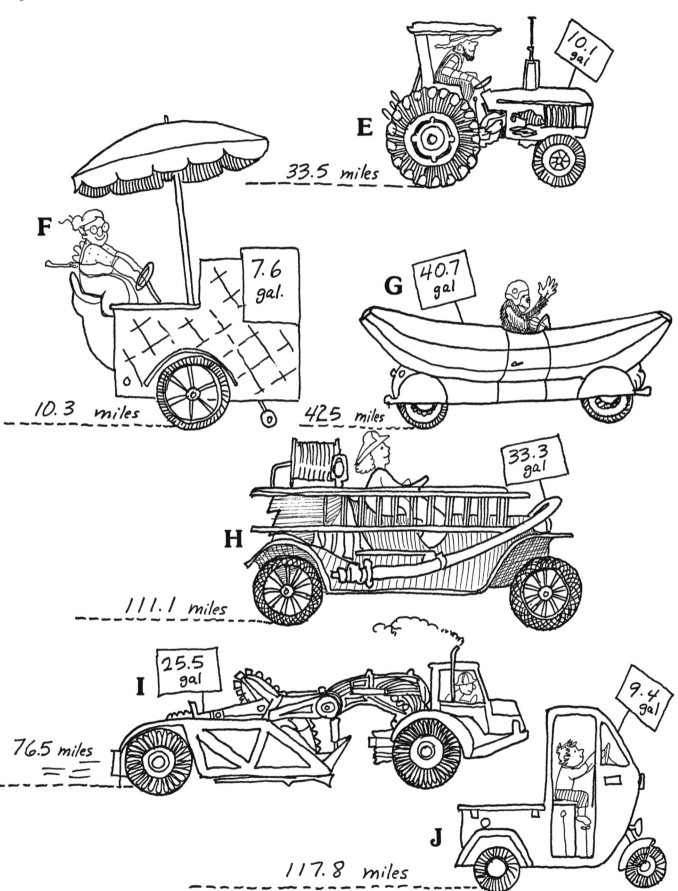

E   10.1 gal

33.5 miles

F   7.6 gal.

10.3 miles

G   40.7 gal

425 miles

H   33.3 gal

111.1 miles

I   25.5 gal

76.5 miles

J   9.4 gal

117.8 miles

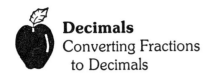

MAKE MINE RHUBARB

Preparation:
- Gather a supply of colored paper, drawing paper, scissors, glue, rulers, compasses, and paper plates.

Use:
1) Talk about favorite kinds of pie. Have students work together to make a list of kinds of pies. Write the list on the chalkboard.
2) Use art supplies to make pies. Have each student design and create a pie.
3) When the pies are finished, instruct the students to divide the pies into equal parts (as large as halves or as small as twelfths). On each piece of pie, students should write the fraction that represents the size of the piece.
4) Give each student a paper plate. Display the pies and allow time for each student to select one or two pieces of pie.
5) Students should write a decimal that represents the fractional amount on each piece of pie.

RATIO,
PROPORTION & PERCENT

RECORD HEIGHTS

Preparation:
- Gather these supplies: mural paper, paints, brushes, tape, encyclopedias, atlases.

Use:
1) Have students draw, paint, and cut out shapes to make a display of snowcapped mountains to put on a bulletin board or wall. (To save time, you can do this ahead of time.)
2) Use encyclopedias and atlases to locate the names and heights of several of the world's highest mountains. Label the names and heights on the display.
3) Ask students to write ratios using this information. (Tell them to round each answer to the nearest hundred.)

   What is the ratio of Mt. Kilimanjaro's height to Mt. McKinley's height?

   What is the ratio of Mt. Whitney's height to Mt. Everest's height?

4) Ask students to devise ratio problems for classmates to solve.

Name _____

COMPARED TO A MOUSE

The giant mouse below is not a mouse of ordinary proportions! As you can see, these jungle animals are not their usual sizes, either. By using ratio, you can determine how the jungle animals compare in size to the mouse.

Ratio is found by dividing one size by another. It can be expressed as a fraction or a decimal.

Write each ratio (problems 1-4) as a fraction in lowest terms.

The lion is 1/2 or 0.5 the size of the mouse.

$$\frac{LION}{MOUSE} = \frac{5'}{10'} = \frac{1}{2} \text{ or } \frac{5}{10} \text{ or } 0.5$$

LION
5'

MOUSE
10'

KANGAROO
4.5'

PARROT
1'

GIRAFFE
9'

APE
6.5'

HIPPO
5.5'

TIGER
4.8'

PYTHON
3'

ZEBRA
6'

1. $\dfrac{\text{Kangaroo}}{\text{Mouse}}$ 2. $\dfrac{\text{Parrot}}{\text{Mouse}}$ 3. $\dfrac{\text{Ape}}{\text{Mouse}}$ 4. $\dfrac{\text{Tiger}}{\text{Mouse}}$

Write each ratio as a decimal (5 - 8).

5. $\dfrac{\text{Giraffe}}{\text{Mouse}}$ 6. $\dfrac{\text{Hippo}}{\text{Mouse}}$ 7. $\dfrac{\text{Python}}{\text{Mouse}}$ 8. $\dfrac{\text{Zebra}}{\text{Mouse}}$

Answers on page 239.

Answers on page 239.

Student Page

Ratio
Rate

HOW DO YOU RATE?

Preparation:
- Ahead of time, formulate several questions that will encourage students to solve rate problems involving situations in the classroom. (See examples below.)

Use:
1) Explain rate and unit rate to students using a classroom example.

RATE is a ratio that is used to compare quantities of different kinds. If there are 754 students in the school and 29 teachers, the number of students per teacher is a ratio:

$$\frac{\text{number of students}}{\text{number of teachers}}$$

UNIT RATE — To find the number of students per teacher, you must find an equal ratio with a denominator of 1.

$$\frac{754 \text{ students}}{29 \text{ teachers}} = \frac{26 \text{ students}}{1 \text{ teacher}}$$

There are 26 students to every teacher.

2) Work with students to figure other rates such as:

- 24 students, 4 art tables
- 168 pieces of paper, 24 students
- 113,100 hot lunches served in a year, 754 students
- 1685 Band-Aids used, 754 students
- 27 classrooms, 3 hallways

3) Students may solve more rate problems by creating their own and/or by completing the student page "Airport Ratios."

Teacher Page

Name _____

AIRPORT RATIOS

There are some problems to be solved at the airport. Find the unit rate for each of these:

1) $2680 for 5 tickets
2) 16 cities in 4 days
3) 9856 miles traveled, 4 travelers
4) 11,076 lbs. of luggage, 213 passengers

5) 27 suitcases, 9 travelers
6) $6324 in tips, 62 skycaps
7) 3335 passengers, 29 planes
8) 966 miles traveled in 3 hrs.
9) 4832 hot dogs, 2416 travelers
10) 110 crew members, 22 planes

Answers on page 239.

Student Page

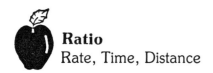

Ratio
Rate, Time, Distance

CATCH A FAST TRAIN

Preparation:
- Gather construction paper, poster board, scissors, markers, paints, glue, and other art supplies for making trains.
- Find books in the library that show various kinds of trains.

Use:
1) Show pictures of different kinds of trains. Provide art supplies for each student to make a train of his or her own design.
2) Explain the relationships among rate, time, and distance. ($D = RT$ $R = \frac{D}{T}$ $T = \frac{D}{R}$)
3) Solve a few problems involving rate, time, and distance.
4) Have each student label his or her train with a name and a speed.
5) Display the trains on a wall or bulletin board and use them for creating and solving rate, time, and distance problems.

Examples:
Which train can travel 680 miles in $1\frac{1}{2}$ hours?
How far will the "Streamin' Demon" travel in 7.8 hours?
How much time will it take each train to go 1000 miles?
How many miles can each train travel in 18 minutes?

The Streamin' Demon goes 75 miles per hour.

Becky R.

Name _____

BIGFOOT CALCULATIONS

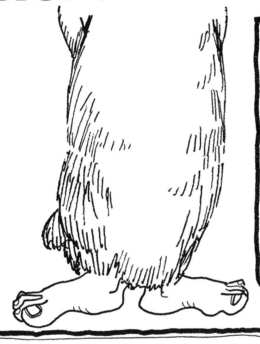

BIGFOOT'S VITAL STATISTICS

HEIGHT........ 7 ft. 6 in.
WEIGHT........ 375 lbs.
FOOTPRINT.....17 in. long
WAIST......... 82 in.
FINGER .... 7 in.
STRIDE....... 5 ft. 9 in.

How does Bigfoot compare to you?
Write a ratio to show how each of Bigfoot's statistics compares to yours.
(Write each fraction or mixed numeral in proper terms.)

Height $\dfrac{\text{Bigfoot's height}}{\text{your height}}$

Weight

Footprint

Waist

Finger

Stride

PROPORTIONATELY SPEAKING

Preparation:
- Fill a bucket with shells, marbles or gum wrappers.

Use:
1) Tell students that some kids picked up the shells (or marbles, gum wrappers, etc.) in 55 minutes. Ask the students to find out how many shells the kids could have collected in 15 minutes.
2) Explain that a proportion can be used to solve such a problem.

A PROPORTION is an equation stating that two ratios are equal.

Write this proportion to solve the problem.

$$\frac{385 \text{ (number of shells)}}{55 \text{ (minutes)}} = \frac{x}{15}$$

x is the number of shells found in 15 minutes.

$$385 \bullet 15 = 55x$$
$$5775 = 55x$$
$$5775 \div 55 = x$$
$$105 = x$$

---

3) Create and solve other proportion problems.

   Example:
   How many shells could the kids have found in 1 hour, 1 minute, or $2\frac{1}{2}$ hours?

4) Give each student a copy of the student page "To Dig A Hole" for more practice solving proportion problems.

Teacher Page

TO DIG A HOLE

These inmates are trying to dig their way out of prison. So far they've dug 17.5 feet in 3 days.

1) How far will they have dug tomorrow?
2) How far will they have dug in three more days?
3) How far had they dug after two days?
4) On what day will they reach 40 feet?
5) How long will it take them to get all the way to the fence?
6) After six days, a group of squirrels filled in 22 feet of the tunnel. Now how long will it take the inmates to finish digging the tunnel?

Answers on page 239.

Student Page

Percentage
Solving Problems

Name _____

SHARP SHOOTERS

Player # 66
Baskets: 4 attempts
          25% success
Free throws: 8 attempts
          75% success

After reading the information below, determine how many points each player scored.
Remember: 1 basket = 2 pts.
            free throw = 1 pt.

Player # 40
Baskets: 20 attempts
          20% success
Free   16 attempts
throws: 75% success

Player # 26
Baskets: 28 attempts
          25% success
Free throws: 5 attempts
          20% success

Player # 81
Baskets: 16 attempts
          100% success
Free throws: 10 attempts
          10% success

Player # 008
Baskets: 35 attempts
          20% success
Free throws: 12 attempts
          75% success

Student Page

Answers on page 239.

102

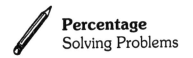

Percentage
Solving Problems

Name _____

WHO'S THE BIG TIPPER?

Who will leave the largest tip?

A. $10.88 10%

B. $27.30 9%

C. $7.55 18%

D. $12.10 11%

E. $16.25 8%

F. $18.66 15%

Answer on page 239.

Student Page

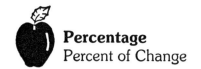

HOW TIMES HAVE CHANGED!

Preparation:
- Make a list of various prices as you remember them 10 years ago. You may find reference materials or colleagues to help you with this. Try to include things that have decreased in price (such as computers, telephones, tape recorders, etc.) as well as things that have increased in price.

Use:
1) Tell students that bread cost about 80 cents (or other appropriate amount) when you were in high school (or other time of your choice). Ask them to determine how much the price of bread has changed since then.
2) Explain that a change (increase or decrease) in an amount may be written as a percent of the original amount (called the percent of change) using this equation:

---

percent of change x original amount = amount of change

or

percent of change = difference between the two amounts / original amount

If bread cost 80 cents then and costs $1.40 now, the price has changed by 60 cents.	Divide 60 by 80 to get .75
	The percent of increase is 75%.

---

3) Give students a list of other prices 10 years ago. Have the students calculate the percent of increase or decrease for each item.

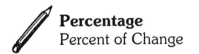

Percentage
Percent of Change

Name _____

UPS & DOWNS

Find the percent of increase or decrease for each situation. (Round to the nearest whole percentage.)

Remember: percent of change = $\dfrac{\text{difference between the two amounts}}{\text{original amount}}$

1) John bought this tent for $77.50 last year. Now it costs $94.55.

2) Rosanna's temperature was 103° yesterday. Now it's 99°.

3) John fell off his skateboard 24 times last week. This week he fell only seven times.

4) The doctor saw 12 cases of chicken pox in February. In April he saw 54 cases.

5) Roberto bought his bike from Jamie for $45.00. He fixed it up and sold it for $52.00.

6) Marie's racing car won a race last year at a speed of 97 miles per hour. This year she won at a speed of 102 miles per hour.

7) Linda bought a robot last year for $72.00. This year the robot costs $80.00.

8) Last year the sixth graders ate a total of 170 pounds of popcorn. This year they ate 195 pounds.

Answers on page 239.

Student Page

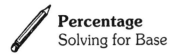

Name _____

IS YOUR HOMEWORK ALMOST DONE?

If you know what percentage of your homework is done and you know the number of pages or problems finished, you can figure out how long the assignment is (the base number) by using an equation.

If you've done 75% of the problems (18 problems), ask yourself:

18 is 75% of what number?	Or 18 = .75 x n
Divide	18 ÷ .75 = n
The assignment is 24 problems.	24 = n

Find the length of each assignment:

1) You've read 26 pages or 50% of the assignment. How long is the assignment?

2) You have studied 90% of the words or 45 words. How many words are there?

3) You have finished 5% or one problem. How long is the assignment?

4) You're on page 215, which is 86% of your book. How long is the book?

5) Twelve or 40% of the sentences are finished. How long is the assignment?

MEASUREMENT

Measurement
Linear/Metric

SCAVENGER HUNT

Preparation:
- Gather metric measuring tools (centimeter rulers, meter sticks, etc.).
- Make up a scavenger hunt which will require students to find things in the room by measuring distances. Prepare and copy a direction sheet such as the example below.

Use:
1) Let students work in pairs or small groups.
2) You might offer a prize or "treasure" for each group that finds all of the items.

Can You Find It?

Two meters from the pencil sharpener is a blue _____.

There are five ____ 2.5 centimeters from the upper right-hand corner of the teacher's desk.

What is located approximately six centimeters below your nose?

_____ is hanging about one meter below the flag.

Nine centimeters to the right of the teacher's right eye is _____.

On your math book cover, what letter is 18 millimeters directly beneath the C in the word "Dictionary"?

Whose classroom is 30.8 meters to the left of ours?

Which of your textbooks is 27 x 15.6 centimeters?

HOW FAR?

Measure to see how far you travel to reach each of these spots from your desk. Write answers in inches, feet, and yards.

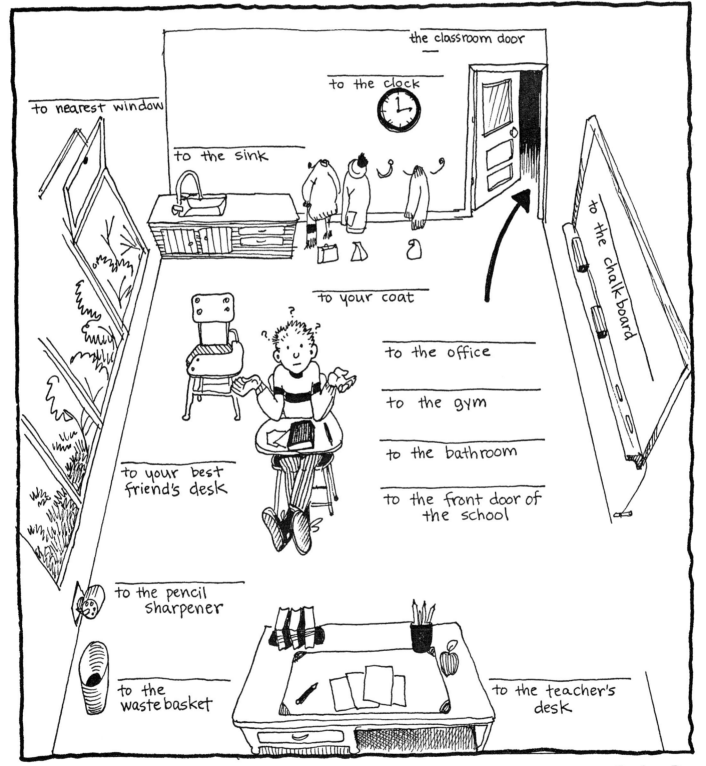

the classroom door

to the clock

to nearest window

to the sink

to the chalkboard

to your coat

to the office _____

to the gym _____

to the bathroom _____

to the front door of the school _____

to your best friend's desk

to the pencil sharpener

to the waste basket

to the teacher's desk

 **Measurement**
Perimeter

Name _____

DANGEROUS CURVES AHEAD

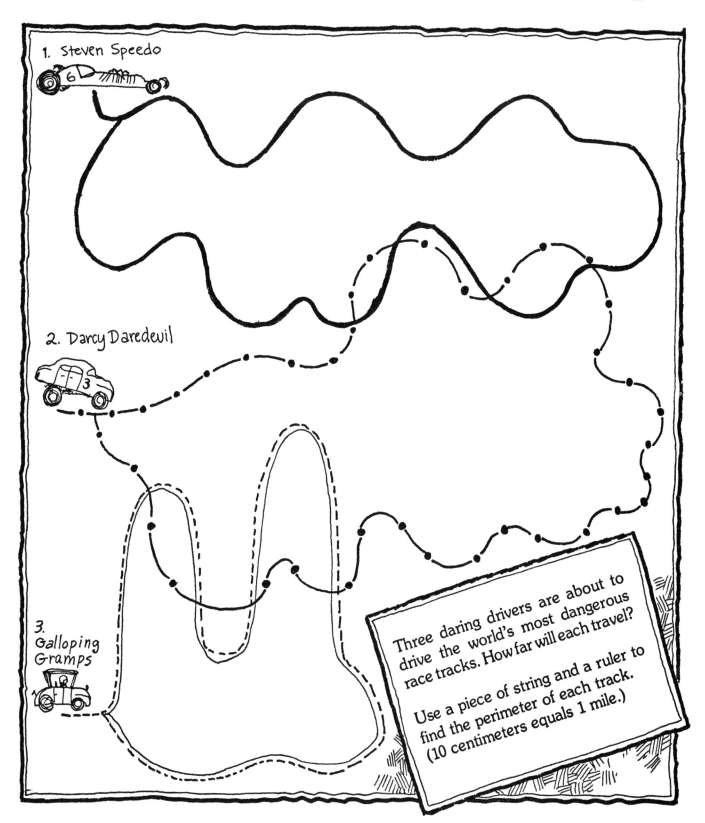

1. Steven Speedo

2. Darcy Daredevil

3. Galloping Gramps

Three daring drivers are about to drive the world's most dangerous race tracks. How far will each travel?

Use a piece of string and a ruler to find the perimeter of each track. (10 centimeters equals 1 mile.)

Name _____

START THE ENGINES

The "Motor Marvels" are about to begin their first annual "motor around the states" marathon.
Measure and compute the distances they will travel.

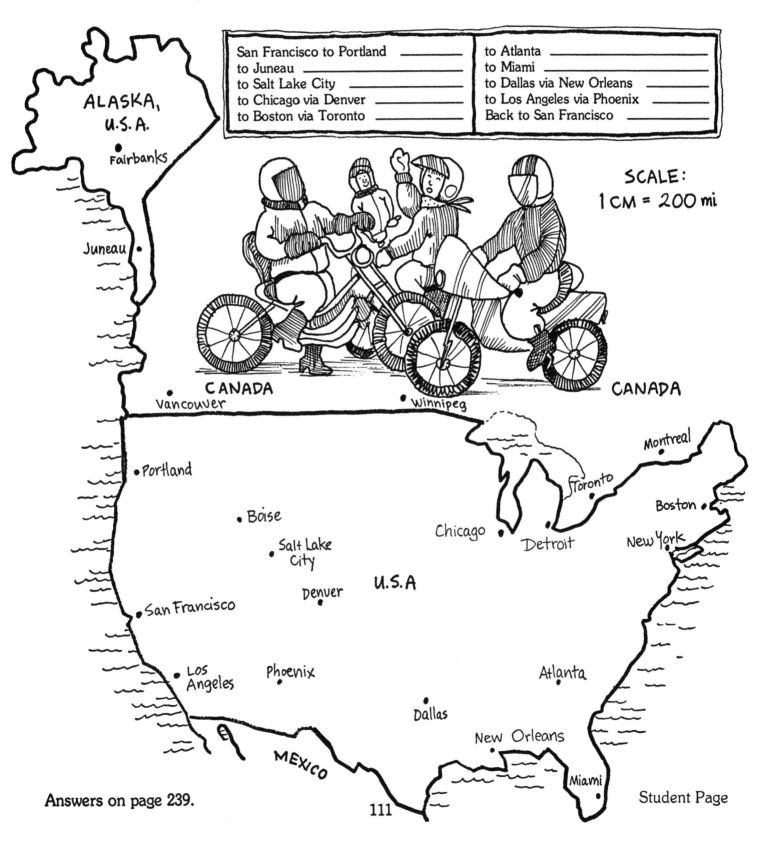

San Francisco to Portland _____   to Atlanta _____
to Juneau _____   to Miami _____
to Salt Lake City _____   to Dallas via New Orleans _____
to Chicago via Denver _____   to Los Angeles via Phoenix _____
to Boston via Toronto _____   Back to San Francisco _____

SCALE:
1 CM = 200 mi

ALASKA, U.S.A.

Fairbanks

Juneau

CANADA

Vancouver

Winnipeg

CANADA

Montreal

Toronto

Portland

Boise

Salt Lake City

Chicago

Detroit

Boston

New York

Denver

U.S.A

San Francisco

Los Angeles

Phoenix

Atlanta

Dallas

New Orleans

MEXICO

Miami

 **Measurement**
Distances

Name _____

PHUNTASTIC PHANTOMLAND

Grover McGulliver Ghost is visiting Phuntastic Phantomland today. Help him get around by calculating the distances he will have to walk (or "float") between adventures.
Invent your own measurement scale on which to base your calculations.

Grover's Route

Screamin' Deamon Roller Coaster
Dracula's Castle
Frankenstein's Fun House

Ghoul Burger Stop
Ferris Werewolf Wheel
Crypt-O-Rama
Zola Zombie's Ice Scream
Bumper Bloodmobiles
Bone Toss
Vampire Rest Stop

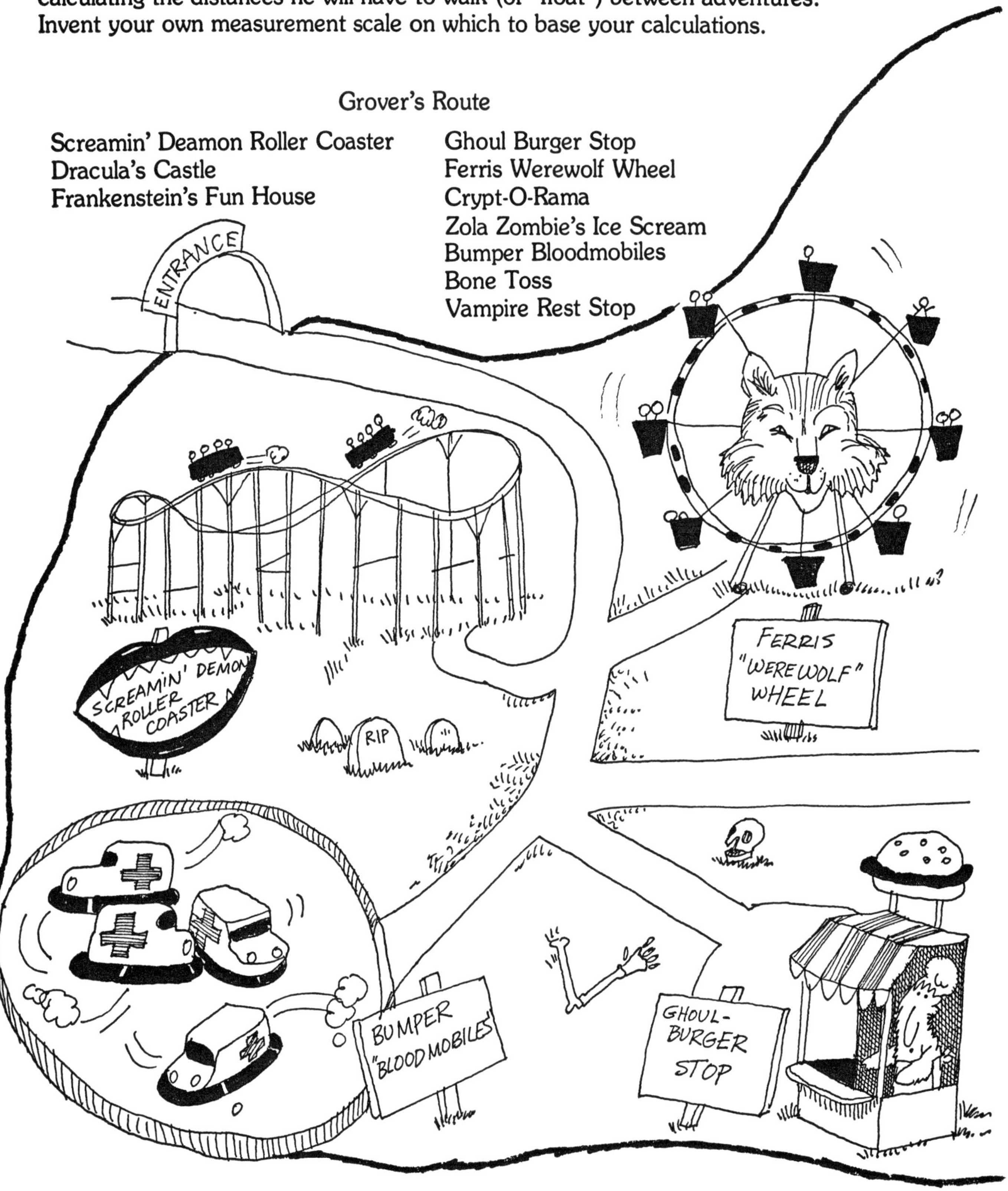

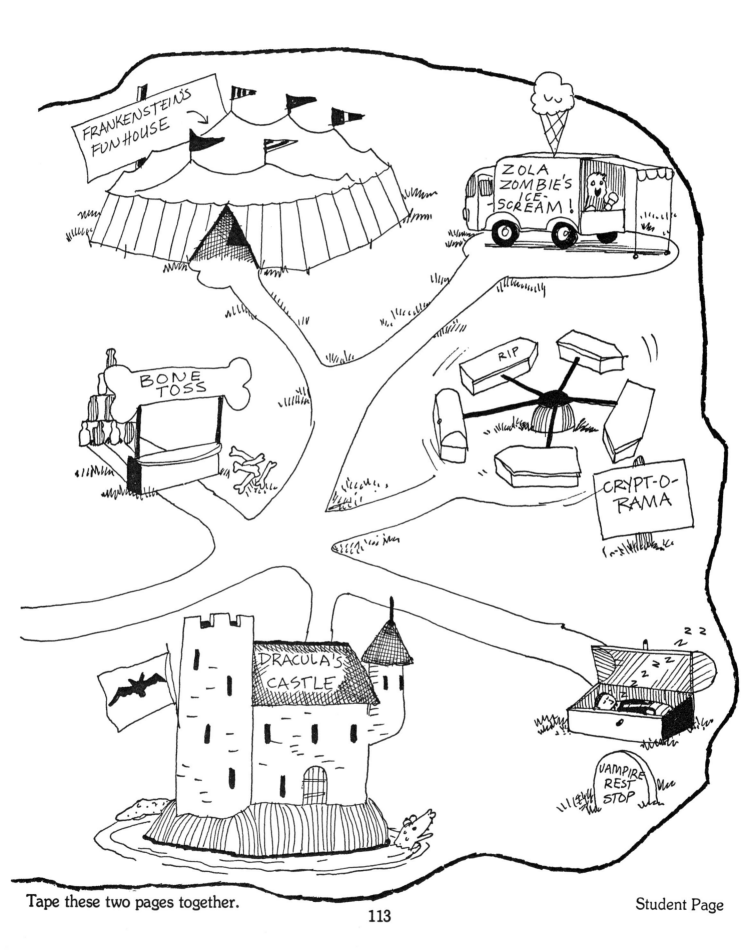

Measurement
Length
Surface Area
Weight

STRAIGHT FROM THE TRASH CAN

Preparation:
- Bring a large, clean trash can to school.
- Collect an assortment of "trash" (clean throwaway objects: old belt, broken toys, empty can, mitten, cardboard mailing tube, empty jug, game, etc.).
- Gather measuring tools for finding length, surface area, and weights of trash items.

Use:
1) Show the trash can to students and tell them you need more clean trash for use in some math activities. Have them bring things from home (no sharp edges).
2) Distribute measuring tools to students and work together to find the length, surface area, and weight for several items. Discuss ways to measure items with unusual shapes (ie: surface area of a shoe). Estimation may help.
3) Allow students to find measurements for some of the items on their own. You may hand out copies of the following student page, or have students create their own charts for record keeping.

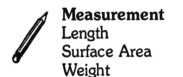

Measurement
Length
Surface Area
Weight

Name _____

KEEPING TRACK OF TRASH

Select 10 trash items and record the following measurements:

TRASH ITEM	LENGTH	SURFACE AREA	WEIGHT

Measure the surface area of three other "trash" items in order to fill in this sentence:

_____ + _____ = _____

AREA SEARCH

Preparation:
- Gather a supply of rulers, yardsticks, meter sticks, and measuring tapes.
- Make enough copies of the student page "Area Mania" for your students.

Use:
1) Review with students the processes and formulas for determining area for a variety of plane figures.
2) Have students refer to the formula chart at the top of the student page "Area Mania."
3) Practice finding a few areas together such as the tops of desks and various shapes drawn on the board.
4) Hand out the "Area Mania" sheets and ask students to find each area in both metric and English measurements. Remind students that the areas must be written in square units.

Area Formulas:
  Circle $A = \pi r^2$ Triangle $A = \frac{1}{2} bh$
  Rectangle $A = bh$ Parallelogram $A = bh$
  Square $A = s^2$ Trapezoid $A = \frac{1}{2} h (b_1 + b_2)$

AREA MANIA

What's the area of ...

1. Your math book?

2. Your ruler?

3. A classroom window?

4. Your kneecap?

5. A wastebasket bottom?

6. A classroom map?

7. The clock?

8. The classroom floor?

9. The bottom of your shoe – approximately?
(Trace on back of this paper.)

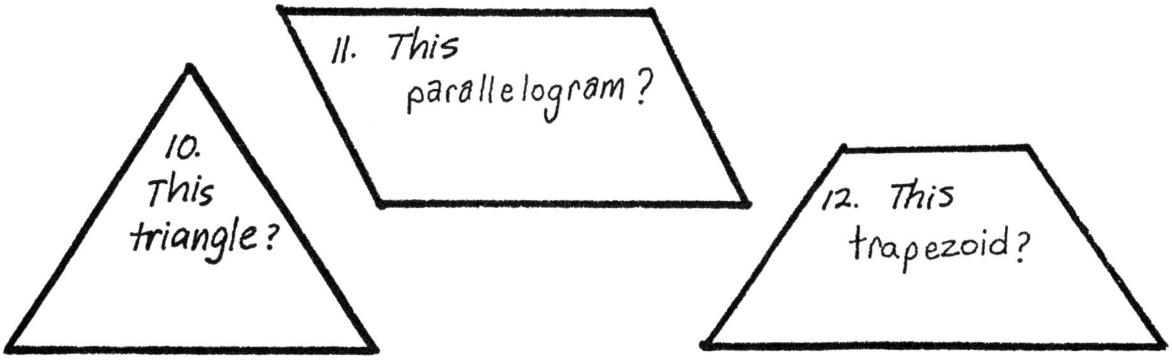

10. This triangle?

11. This parallelogram?

12. This trapezoid?

Student Page

WRAP IT UP!

Preparation:
- Collect several items which represent solid geometric figures — spheres, cones, prisms, cylinders, pyramids, etc. (candle, megaphone, rectangular bubble gum, softball, small balloons, dice, party hats, small boxes, glass prism).
- Have on hand a supply of cellophane tape, aluminum foil, rulers, and single-edged razor blades.

Use:
1) Have students work in pairs to wrap the solid figures with foil, making sure it clings well. Any loose edges may be taped.
2) When figures are well wrapped, help students slit the foil carefully along enough edges to remove the wrapping in one flat piece.
3) Ask the students to find the surface area of each figure by measuring the sections of flattened foil.

Measurement
Angles

Name _____

ANGLER'S PARADISE

Search this scene for angles.

Use your protractor to measure at least 30 angles and write the measurement of each *in the* angle.

Student Page

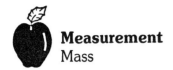

A MASS OF MASS

Preparation:
- Bring a metric scale to class.
- Gather a collection of items that have masses of just a few milligrams to several kilograms.
- Make a copy of the student page "Mastering Mass" for each student.

Use:
1) As a group, practice weighing several items and writing the masses in milligrams, grams, or kilograms.
2) Give each student a copy of the student page "Mastering Mass" and discuss together the chart at the top of the page. Based on this information, make estimates about the mass of several objects in the classroom.
3) Let students work on their own to finish the page.

Note: Mass should not be confused with weight. The mass of an object is a measure of the amount of matter it contains. Weight is a measure of the force of gravity between an object and the earth. The mass of an object would be the same on earth or in space, but its weight would be different. In the metric system, mass is measured in grams, weight is measured in newtons. (Pounds measure weight in the English system.)

Name _____

MASTERING MASS

1 gram (g)	= 1000 milligrams (mg)
1 kilogram (kg)	= 1000 grams (g)
1 metric ton (t)	= 1000 kilograms (kg)

1 milliliter of water has a mass of 1 gram   1 liter of water has a mass of 1 kilogram

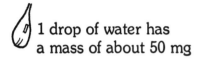 1 drop of water has a mass of about 50 mg

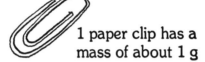 1 paper clip has a mass of about 1 g

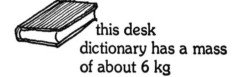 this desk dictionary has a mass of about 6 kg

 1 nickel has a mass of about 5 g

 this school bus has a mass of about 5 t

 1 football has a mass of about 500 g

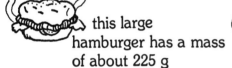 this large hamburger has a mass of about 225 g

 this large watermelon has a mass of about 20 kg

this luxury car has a mass of about 1 t

Determine if each object's mass is more or less than a kilogram. Fill a liter soda pop bottle with water (weight: 1 kg) to help you decide.

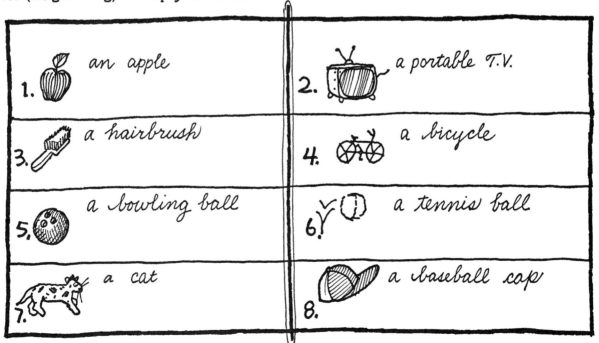

1. an apple

2. a portable T.V.

3. a hairbrush

4. a bicycle

5. a bowling ball

6. a tennis ball

7. a cat

8. a baseball cap

Name _____

OUT OF THIS WORLD

Astronaut Michael Moonrocket weighs 180 pounds on the earth and 30 pounds on the moon.

Find these weights in pounds:

MOON WEIGHT = EARTH'S
WEIGHT DIVIDED BY 6.

1. ASTEROID
   earth weight: 246 lb
   moon weight: _____

2. SPACESHIP
   earth weight: 980,284 lb
   moon weight: _____

3. SMALL MOON
   CREATURE
   earth weight: _____
   moon weight: 2 lb

4. LARGE MOON
   CREATURE
   earth weight: _____
   moon weight: 24 lb

5. MONKEY
   earth weight: 30 lb
   moon weight: _____

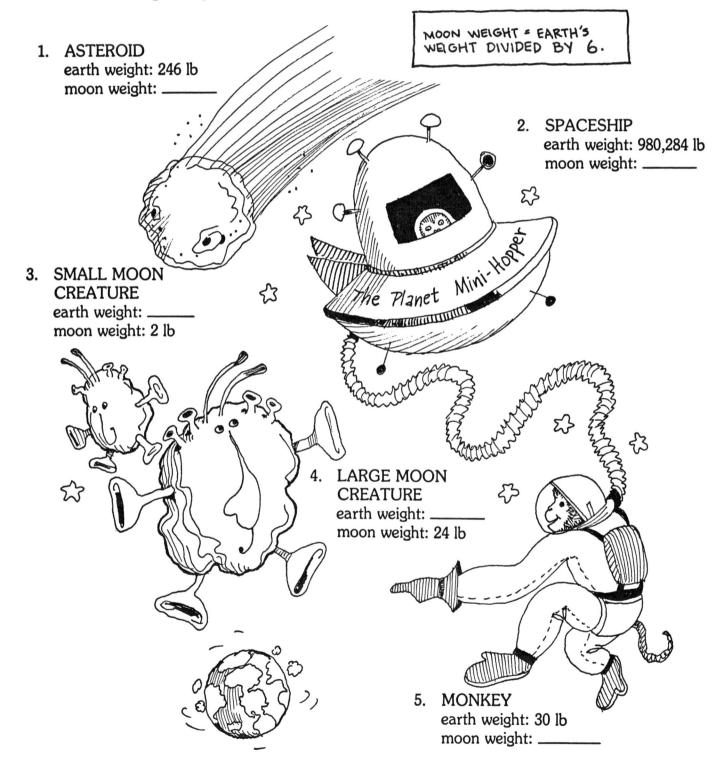

Measurement
Liquid/Dry

FULL OF BEANS

Preparation:
- You will need an old suitcase, enough dry beans to fill it, and containers in these sizes: cup, pint, quart, gallon, liter.
- Fill the suitcase with beans and label each container with the appropriate capacity.
- Create tasks and questions such as these:

1 gal = ____ qts	1 qt = ____ pts
1 pt = ____ cups	1 qt = ____ cups
____ gal = 12 pts	16 cups = ____ gal

Which is more, 2 pts. or 1 liter? _____
Your shoe holds approximately _____ liters.
About how many liters make a gallon? _____

Use:
1) Give students time to visit the suitcase and do the measuring tasks individually. Students may write answers and turn them in as a regular math assignment.
2) Ask students to add at least one more question for other students to answer.

METRIC BREAD

Preparation:
- Gather ingredients as listed in recipes on the following page.
- Plan to begin this activity on a Monday.
- Have on hand a metric scale and calibrated liter container.

Use:
1) On a Monday morning, have students prepare the "Metric Sourdough Starter."
2) Make a schedule which allows everyone to take turns stirring three times daily over the next five days.
3) On Friday afternoon, refrigerate the starter.
4) The following Monday, follow the directions for making "Metric Sourdough Bread."
5) Enjoy eating the bread with butter and jam!

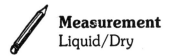

METRIC SOURDOUGH STARTER

7 g	dry yeast (1 package)
625 mL	warm water
500 mL	flour (white or part white, part wheat)
20 mL	sugar

1. Dissolve yeast in 200 mL warm water.
2. Stir in remaining water, flour, and sugar.
3. Cover with paper towel or plastic wrap.
4. Let stand in a warm spot in the room for five days.
5. Stir the mixture three times daily.

METRIC SOURDOUGH BREAD

7 g	dry yeast (1 package)
375 mL	warm water
250 mL	sourdough starter
15 mL	salt
20 mL	sugar
5 mL	baking soda
1400 mL	flour

1. Soften yeast in warm water.
2. Add starter, salt, sugar and 600 mL flour. Beat well for five minutes.
3. Cover. Let rise until bubbly (1-2 hours).
4. Mix 600 mL flour with baking soda and stir into dough.
5. Add enough extra flour to make a stiff dough.
6. Knead for 10 minutes onto a floured surface.
7. Divide the dough in half and let it rise 10 minutes.
8. Shape two loaves and place on a greased baking sheet.
9. Cut diagonal slashes across the top.
   Bake in 400° oven for about 35 minutes.

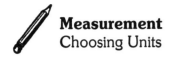

Measurement
Choosing Units

Name _____

HOW TO MEASURE AN ELEPHANT

Write the metric unit of measure that you would use for each situation below. (Don't forget to write square or cubic units when needed.)

1. frosting needed for a cake...

unit: _____

2. choosing a box to mail a skateboard...

unit: _____

3. paint for your bedroom...

unit: _____

4. water to fill a swimming pool...

unit: _____

5. the distance around an elephant...

unit: _____

6. dividing a pizza...

unit: _____

7. pole vaulting...

unit: _____

8. deciding if a lake is deep enough for diving...

unit: _____

9. wrapping a Christmas present...

unit: _____

10. the distance to Disneyland...

unit: _____

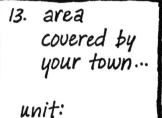

INTERSTATE 1000

MIDTOWN, USA

PARTWAY

11. serving cola to friends...

unit: _____

12. weight of a friend...

unit: _____

UH OH!

13. area covered by your town...

unit: _____

14. how far you can throw a softball...

unit: _____

squawk!

15. amount of milkshake you can drink...

unit: _____

I CAN'T BELIEVE I DRANK THE WHOLE THING!

Answers on page 239.

Student Page

TIME OUT

Preparation:
- Have students use poster board to make large clocks or watches. Students may draw clock hands to specify a particular time on each clock. (Digital times may be shown, too.)
- Give each watch or clock a letter name.
- Hang the time pieces from the ceiling at the front of the room.

Use:
1) Choose one clock and ask the class what time it will be in one hour.
2) Ask other questions such as, "Which clock tells us it's twenty-seven past three?"
3) Give each student a copy of the student page "It's About Time!" Ask each student to choose one clock and answer the questions on the student page.

Name _____

IT'S ABOUT TIME!

Choose one of the clocks hanging in the room.

Clock name or letter: _____
Clock time: _____

Answer these questions using the chosen clock.

What time was it 1 hour and 15 minutes ago? _____

How much time in hours and minutes will pass before lunch?

_____

How long ago was it 8:12 a.m.? _____

What will the time be in 6½ hours? _____

How much time is left until the end of the school day?

_____

What time was it 10 hours and 36 minutes before the time on

your clock? _____

What is your favorite time of day? _____

How long will it be until your favorite time of day?

(Or how long ago was it?) _____

What time was it 57 minutes ago? _____

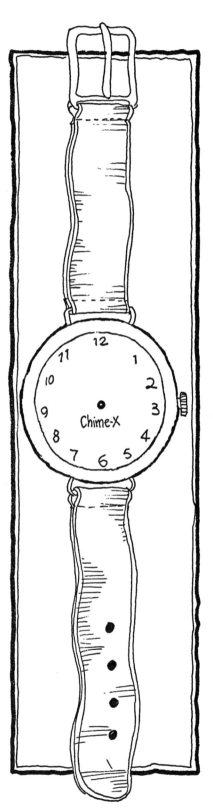

Measurement
Metric Scale

GROW, LITTLE GROWBUG!

Make this little metric growbug grow much larger.

Each square is 1 square centimeter. The grid below has the same number of squares, but each one is four times as large (2 cm. sq.).

To make the bug grow, copy the bug onto the large grid, drawing one square at a time.

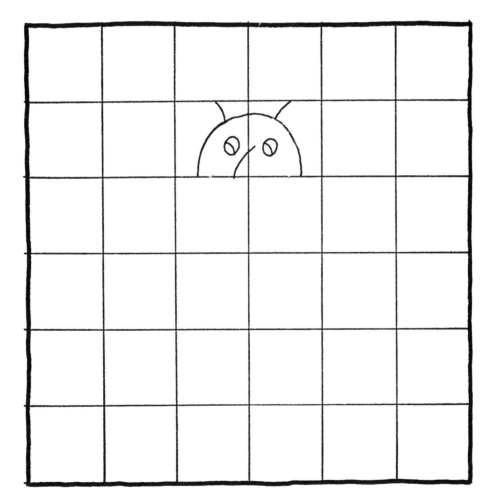

You can make this growbug grow even more! Draw a diagram with six rows of six squares, each 4 centimeters square, and copy the growbug again.

Student Page

130

GEOMETRY

YOU DON'T NEED A CHAIN SAW

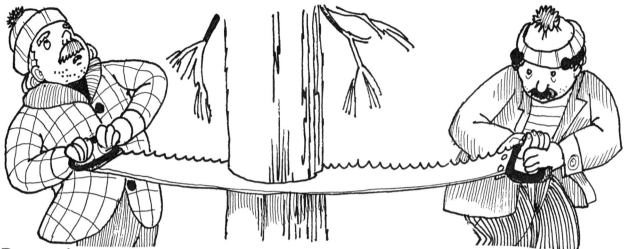

Preparation:
- Have compasses, rulers, and drawing paper available for students.

Use:
1) Explain to students that dividing a line segment into two equal or congruent parts is called bisecting the line segment. The line that bisects another is called a bisector.
2) Have students follow these dictated directions for making a perpendicular bisector.

- Draw a horizontal line 10 cm long across the center of your paper. Label it A (left end) B (right end).
- Open your compass to a radius greater than 5 cm.
- Using A as the center, draw a circle.
- Using B as the center, draw a circle.
- Find the spot above the line where the circles intersect. Label this point X. Label the intersection below the line Y.
- Draw the line $\overline{XY}$. Label the point where $\overline{XY}$ intersects $\overline{AB}$ point M. M is the midpoint of $\overline{AB}$. $\overline{XY}$ is the perpendicular bisector of $\overline{AB}$.

3) The completed constructions should look like this.

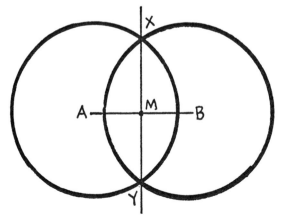

Name _____

WHAT'S MY LINE?

Try to identify and name each kind of line described below.

A. I am part of a line that has two endpoints.

B.
The two of us meet and cross each other.

C.
When I meet another line, it is always at a right angle.

D.
I'm a part of a line that has an endpoint at only one end.

E.
I extend in opposite directions without end.

F.
I am made of two rays that have the same endpoint.

G.
We are lines in the same plane, but we've never met.

Answers on page 239.

Student Page

WHICH FIGURE IS WHICH?

___ 1. trapezoid

___ 2. scalene triangle

___ 3. obtuse triangle

___ 4. rectangle

___ 5. triangle

___ 6. octagon

___ 7. polygon

___ 8. pentagon

___ 9. square

___ 10. hexagon

___ 11. isosceles triangle

___ 12. equilateral triangle

___ 13. rhombus

___ 14. parallelogram

___ 15. quadrilateral

___ 16. right triangle

A. A figure which is made up of line segments called sides and is joined at endpoints called vertices

B. A plane figure with three angles and three sides

C. A triangle with two equal sides and two equal angles

D. A triangle with no equal sides and no equal angles

E. A triangle with one right angle

F. A triangle with all sides and all angles equal

G. A triangle with one obtuse angle

H. A polygon with four sides

I. A quadrilateral whose opposite sides are parallel

J. A parallelogram with four right angles

K. A parallelogram with four equal sides

L. A rectangle with four equal sides

M. A quadrilateral with only one pair of parallel sides

N. A five-sided polygon

O. A six-sided polygon

P. An eight-sided polygon

Name _____

WHERE HAS POLY-GON?

Find each of these figures hidden in the puzzle below. Color each figure as directed. You may use the completed and checked student page "Which Figure Is Which?" to help you.

(1) octagon - dk. blue
(2) obtuse triangle - tan
(3) isosceles triangle - lt. blue
(1) pentagon - grey
(1) trapezoid - yellow

(1) rhombus - green
(1) hexagon - pink
(2) right triangle - brown
(1) rectangle - lavendar
(1) parallelogram - orange

(4) quadrilateral - purple
(1) square - black
(2) equilateral triangle - aqua

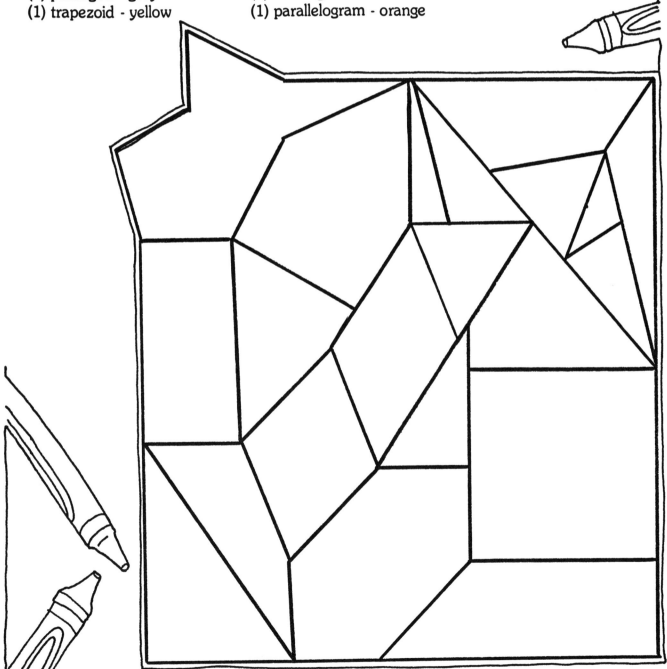

Student Page

Geometry
Circles

CIRCULAR FACTS

Preparation:
- Gather enough compasses and rulers for your class.

Use:
1) Discuss with students the description of a circle and other geometric terms related to it. You may give each student a copy of the chart below or have students write the information in a notebook.
2) Find examples of circles, radii, arcs, chords, tangents, central angles, diameters, etc. in the room or in pictures.
3) Give each student a copy of the student page "Finding Your Way Around A Circle." Allow time for the class to complete the activity and share the results.

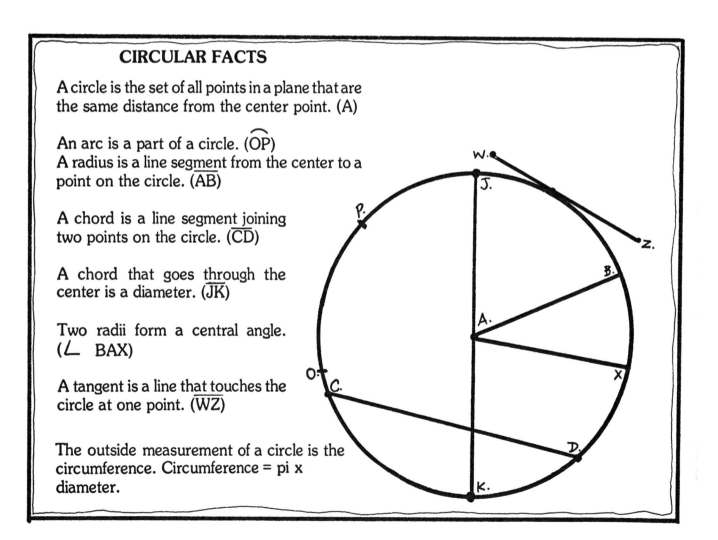

CIRCULAR FACTS

A circle is the set of all points in a plane that are the same distance from the center point. (A)

An arc is a part of a circle. ($\overset{\frown}{OP}$)
A radius is a line segment from the center to a point on the circle. ($\overline{AB}$)

A chord is a line segment joining two points on the circle. ($\overline{CD}$)

A chord that goes through the center is a diameter. ($\overline{JK}$)

Two radii form a central angle. ($\angle$ BAX)

A tangent is a line that touches the circle at one point. ($\overline{WZ}$)

The outside measurement of a circle is the circumference. Circumference = pi x diameter.

FINDING YOUR WAY AROUND A CIRCLE

I'VE BEEN GOING IN CIRCLES FOR YEARS!

Design and draw an invention of your own. Make sure it contains the following:

> at least four circles of different sizes
> 1 or more radii
> three chords
> two diameters
> five arcs
> two central angles
> one tangent

Invention ideas: vehicle, machine, timesaving device, home-entertainment center, exercise equipment, etc.

POLYHEDRA HUNT

Preparation:
- Gather as many objects as possible which represent the space figures identified below and hide them in inconspicuous places around the room.

Use:
1) Review with students the descriptions of the polyhedra below.
2) Give each student a copy of the student page "In Search Of The Elusive Polyhedra."
3) Set a specific amount of time for students to search for the hidden objects in pairs or small groups. Ask students to locate and name as many polyhedra as possible in the allotted time.
4) As students discover a polyhedron, they should record and describe it on the student page.

Prism: has two congruent, parallel bases. The bases may be triangles, squares, rectangles, hexagons, etc.

Pyramid: has at least three faces that are triangles. The base may be a triangle, square, pentagon, or other shape.

Cube: is a prism with three sets of parallel bases, all being congruent squares.

Cone: has a flat, circular base and one vertex.

Cylinder: has two congruent, parallel circular bases.

Sphere: a space figure in which all of the points on its surface are the same distance from its center.

Name _____

IN SEARCH OF THE ELUSIVE POLYHEDRA

Keep a record of each polyhedron you find:

Name of Object	Name of Polyhedron	How do you know which polyhedron the object is?

Name _____

BEHIND CLOSED DOORS

A space figure is hiding behind each door. Use the clues on each door to determine which of these figures is hidden there.

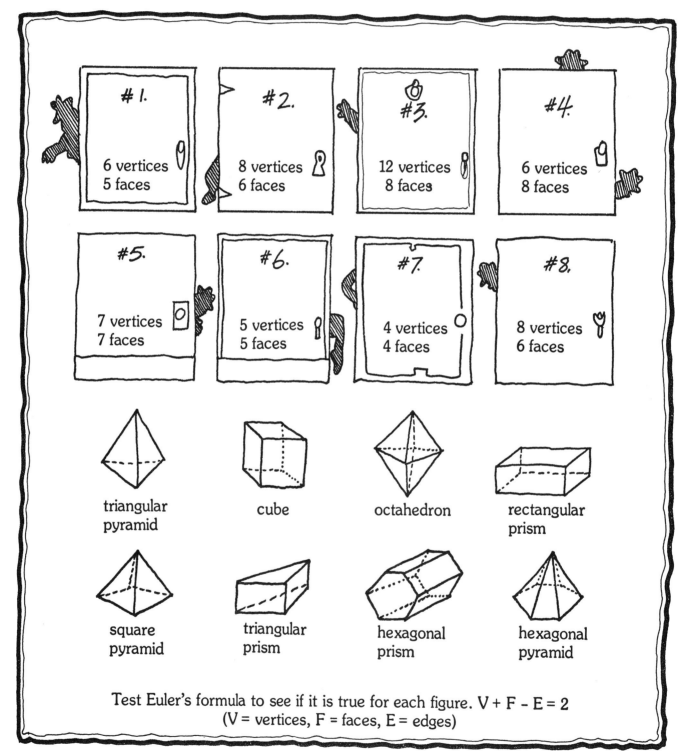

#1.
6 vertices
5 faces

#2.
8 vertices
6 faces

#3.
12 vertices
8 faces

#4.
6 vertices
8 faces

#5.
7 vertices
7 faces

#6.
5 vertices
5 faces

#7.
4 vertices
4 faces

#8.
8 vertices
6 faces

triangular pyramid

cube

octahedron

rectangular prism

square pyramid

triangular prism

hexagonal prism

hexagonal pyramid

Test Euler's formula to see if it is true for each figure. V + F − E = 2
(V = vertices, F = faces, E = edges)

Name _____

HOLD EVERYTHING!

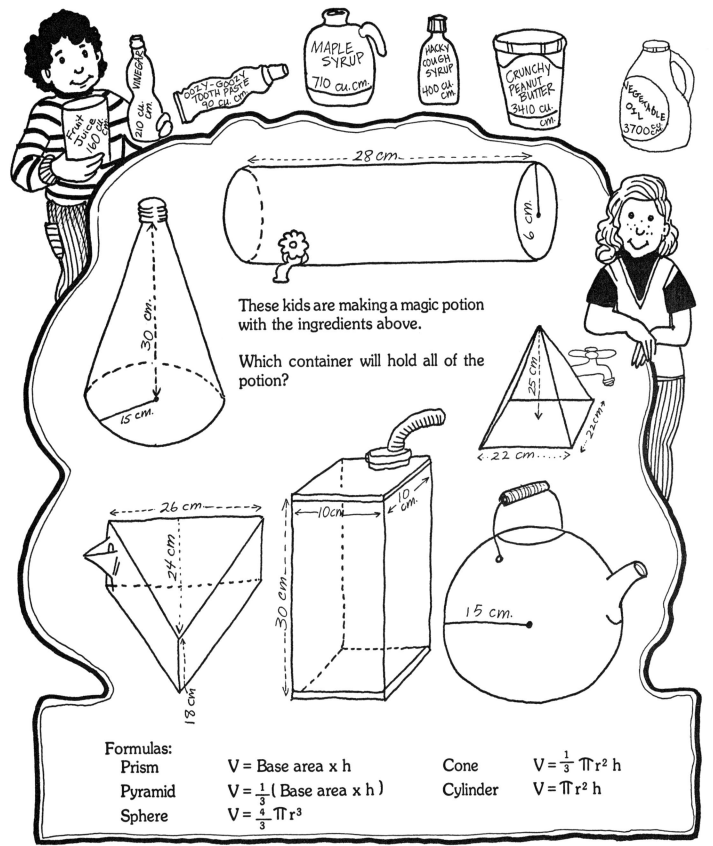

These kids are making a magic potion with the ingredients above.

Which container will hold all of the potion?

Labels on ingredients:
- VINEGAR 210 cu. cm.
- OOZY-GOOZY TOOTH PASTE 90 cu. cm.
- MAPLE SYRUP 710 cu. cm.
- HACKY COUGH SYRUP 400 cu. cm.
- CRUNCHY PEANUT BUTTER 3410 cu. cm.
- VEGETABLE OIL 3700 cu. cm.
- Fruit Juice 160 cu. cm.

Cylinder: 28 cm, 6 cm
Cone: 30 cm., 15 cm.
Pyramid: 25 cm, 22 cm, 22 cm
Prism: 26 cm, 24 cm, 18 cm
Rectangular prism: 10 cm, 10 cm, 30 cm
Sphere: 15 cm.

Formulas:
Prism	V = Base area x h	Cone	$V = \frac{1}{3} \pi r^2 h$
Pyramid	$V = \frac{1}{3}$ (Base area x h)	Cylinder	$V = \pi r^2 h$
Sphere	$V = \frac{4}{3} \pi r^3$		

ANGLES AWAY

Preparation:

- Make enough copies of the student page "Always Another Angle" for each student.
- Have drawing paper, pencils, protractors, and rulers available for students.

Use:

1) Use the student page "Always Another Angle" for teaching or reviewing the descriptions of various kinds of angles. Ask students to look for other examples of each angle in the picture or around the room.

2) Give students drawing paper, pencils, protractors, and rulers, and dictate the following directions:

   a) Draw a house that has one acute angle and one obtuse angle.
   b) Draw a vehicle that contains two pairs of adjacent angles.
   c) Draw a skateboard with four straight angles.
   d) Draw a toy with no right angles.
   e) Draw a design with two supplementary angles and two complementary angles.
   f) Draw a hat with a pair of vertical angles.
   g) Draw a dessert with a straight angle.

Geometry
Angles

Name _____

ALWAYS ANOTHER ANGLE

Find one or more examples of each angle in the picture above.

acute angle — measures more than 0°, less than 90°
right angle — measures 90°
adjacent angles — have a common vertex and side
complementary angles — two angles whose sum is 90°
vertical angles — pairs of opposite angles formed when two lines intersect
obtuse angle — more than 90°, less than 180°
straight angle — measures 180°
congruent angles — two angles that measure the same
supplementary angles — two angles whose sum is 180°

Student Page

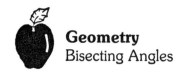

A SLICE OF A SLICE

Preparation:
- You will need drawing paper, crayons, rulers, compasses, and protractors.

Use:
1) Ask each student to draw and lightly color a slice of pizza that forms an angle of less than 90°.
2) Tell students that they must divide their slices exactly in half by performing the process called bisecting an angle.

- Label the vertex of the angle E. Label the left leg of the angle D at the top end. Label the end of the lower leg F. This forms ∠ DEF.
- With E as center of the circle, use your compass to draw an arc which intersects $\overline{ED}$ and $\overline{EF}$.
- Label the point of intersection on $\overline{ED}$ point G and the point of intersection on $\overline{EF}$ point H.
- Open your compass to a radius greater than half the distance between G and H. Using G and H as centers, draw two arcs that intersect $\overline{ED}$ and $\overline{EF}$.
- Find the point where these two arcs intersect. Label this point O.
- Draw line $\overline{EO}$. This is the bisector of ∠ DEF. Now you should have two pieces of pizza of the exact same size (∠ DEO and ∠ OEF). Measure the angles with your protractor to be sure.

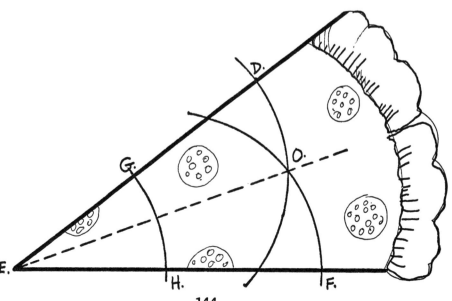

"REFLECTING YOURSELF"

A figure is symmetric if a line (real or imaginary) divides it into two congruent (equal) parts which fit together exactly when folded on the line.

You can write your name in a symmetric design.

Follow these directions:

1) Fold a piece of colored construction paper (11" x 17") in half lengthwise.

2) Write your name in large cursive letters along the fold line with a piece of chalk. (Write lightly.)

   Important: The letters should reach almost to the top of the paper.

   If your name has a letter with a "tail," leave the tail off. (See the j and the f in Jennifer.)

   The bottom of each letter must touch the fold and all letters must be connected.

3) Fold the paper so that the writing faces the outside. Cut around your name, not on the line but away from it, to make large, fat letters. Cut out the centers of any letters such as o, e, d, etc.

4) Gently wipe off the chalk. Open the design and glue it onto a piece of paper of a contrasting color.

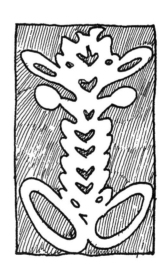

Name _____

MY NEXT BIRTHDAY PRESENT

Graph these points on the grid on the next page and connect the dots to find a spectacular birthday present. Graph the sequence of ordered pairs group by group. After graphing all of the points in group A, connect the dots in the order you graphed them. (Be sure to connect every dot.) Do this for each group of ordered pairs.

A	B	C	D	E
(2,–6)	(4,–3)	$(-4\frac{1}{2},-4\frac{1}{2})$	(–2,2)	(2,8)
(1,–9)	(4,–1)	(–6,–4)	(–2,–2)	(3,7)
(3,–9)	(3,0)	(–6,–3)	(2,–2)	(3,5)
(3,–8)	(5,–6)	(–5,0)	(2,2)	(2,4)
(4,–8)	(–5,–6)	(–4,1)		(–2,4)
(4,–10)	(–3,0)	(–5,1)		(–3,5)
(–4,–10)	(–4,–1)	(–5,4)		(–3,7)
(–4,–8)	(–4,–3)	(–3,4)		(–2,8)
(–3,–8)		(–3,3)		(2,8)
(–3,–9)		(3,3)		
(–1,–9)		(3,4)		
(–2,–6)		(5,4)		
		(5,1)		
		(4,1)		
		(5,0)		
		(6,–3)		
		(6,–4)		
		$(4\frac{1}{2}, -4\frac{1}{2})$		

I THINK HE'S REALLY GOING TO BE SURPRISED THIS YEAR!

HAPPY BIRTHDAY, SON

Name _____

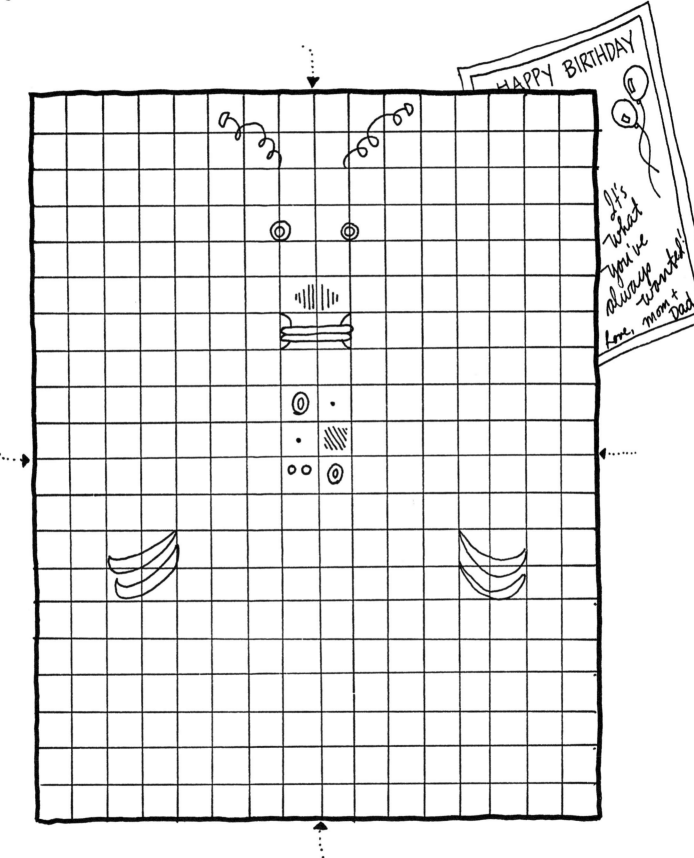

POINT, COUNTERPOINT

Preparation:
- Supply students with graph paper and rulers.

Use:

1) Have each student construct a grid with four quadrants, numbering both the X and Y axes.

2) Dictate the following pairs of coordinates. Tell students that they are to plot and label the points as you dictate.

(0, –10)	(5, –6)	(8,0)	(5,6)	(0,10)
(–5,6)	(–8,0)	(–5,–6)		

3) Instruct students to connect the points with straight lines and identify the geometric figure (an octagon).

4) Students may then create their own "secret" figures and dictate coordinates to one another to identify the figures.

DO-IT-YOURSELF SPACE FIGURES

Preparation:
- Make copies of the following five pattern pages for your class.
- Students will need crayons, markers, scissors, and glue or tape.

Use:
1) As a beginning or a culmination for a lesson on space figures, spend a math class period making your own. The following patterns will allow students to easily construct five of the most common polyhedra.

2) Have students make the five figures by following the printed directions. You may give students time to color or decorate the figures before taping or gluing them together.

3) Use the completed figures for a variety of lessons. For example:
- count numbers of faces, edges, vertices
- find surface area of each figure
- figure volume of each

Name _____

Cut along the solid lines.
Fold on the dotted lines.
Tape the tabs together to make a cube.

How square can you get!

My Name is:

Cube Jr.

Cube Pattern

Geometry
Space Figures

Name _____

Rectangle Man

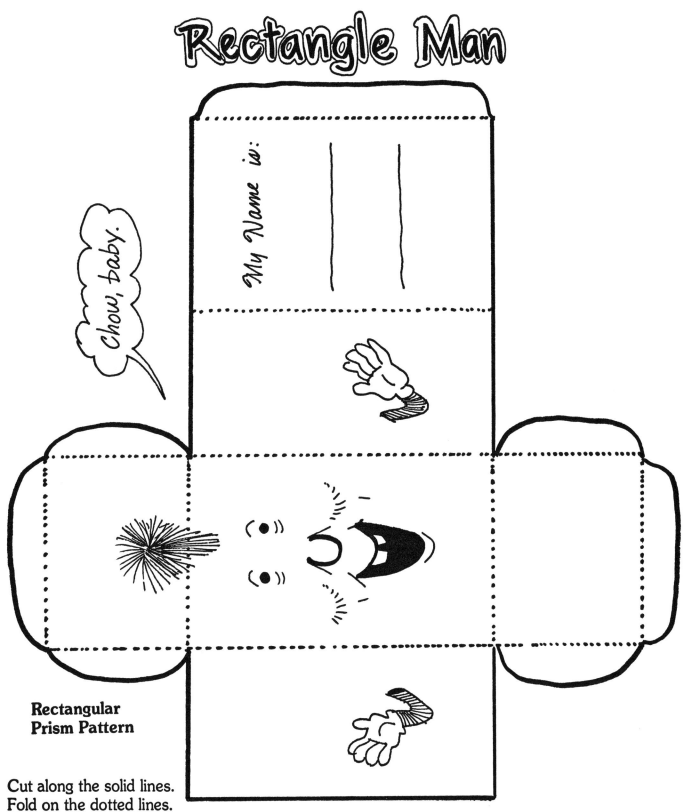

**Rectangular
Prism Pattern**

Cut along the solid lines.
Fold on the dotted lines.
Tape the tabs together to make a rectangular prism.

151

Student Page

Geometry
Space Figures

Name _____

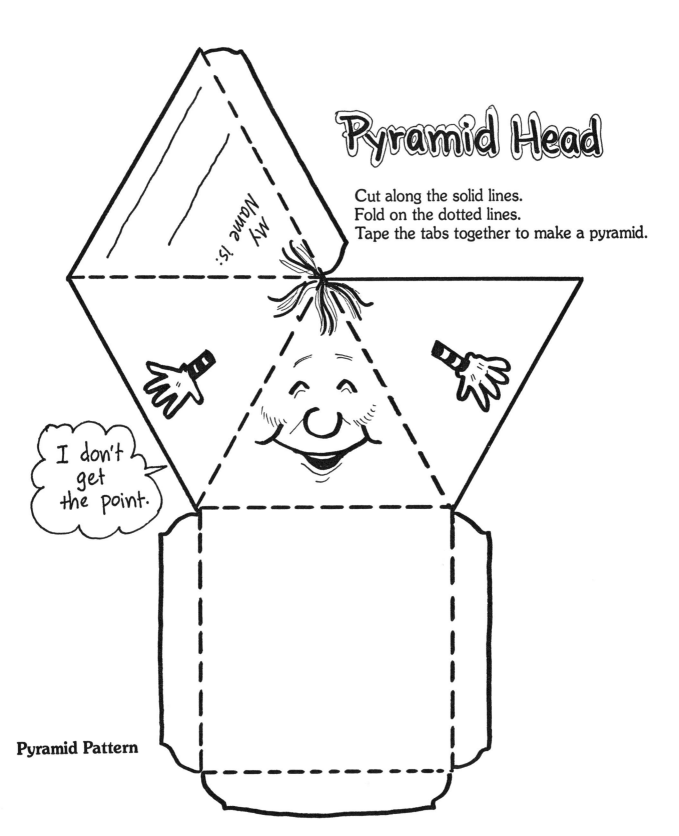

Pyramid Head

Cut along the solid lines.
Fold on the dotted lines.
Tape the tabs together to make a pyramid.

My Name is:

I don't get the point.

Pyramid Pattern

Cylinder-ella

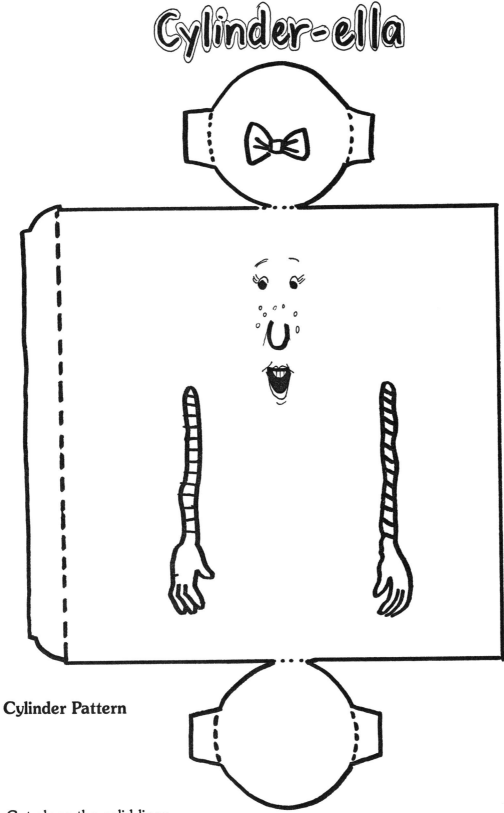

Cylinder Pattern

Cut along the solid lines.
Fold on the dotted lines.
Tape the tabs together to make a cylinder.

Geometry
Space Figures

Name _____

Cut along the solid lines.
Fold on the dotted lines.
Tape the tabs together to make a cone.

Cone-y

Cone Pattern

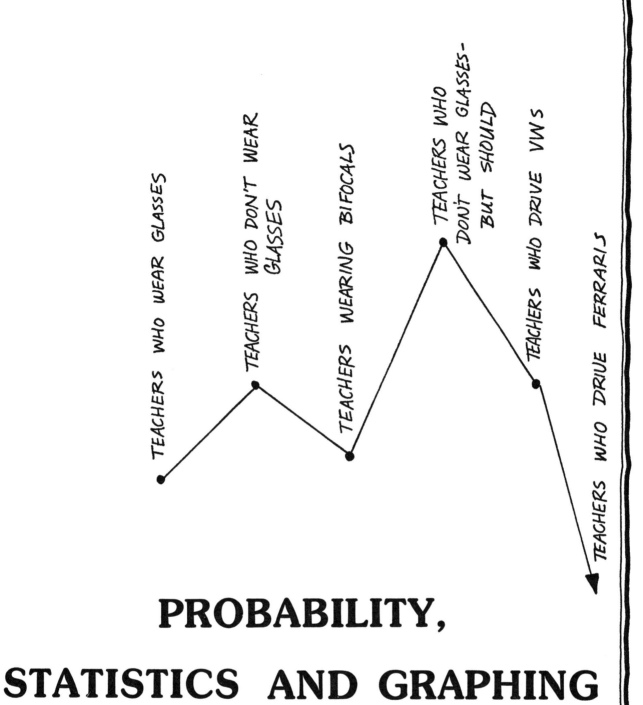

PROBABILITY,
STATISTICS AND GRAPHING

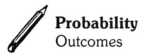

Name _____

PROBABLY PISTACHIO

The Big Dipper ice cream shop serves 35 flavors. If the attendant dips out one scoop of ice cream with his or her eyes closed, what is the chance it will be pistachio?

Because there are 35 flavors, there are 35 possible outcomes.

Because the attendant is choosing without looking, all of the outcomes are equally likely.

There is one chance in 35 that the scoop will be pistachio. So, the probability of getting pistachio is 1 in 35 or 1/35.

For each of the examples on these pages, write the probability in fraction form.

a) Toss a penny. Probability of heads: _____

1 cent

b) Wearing a blindfold, draw one ball from the box. Probability of stripes: _____

c) Spin the spinner. Probability of landing on green:

_____

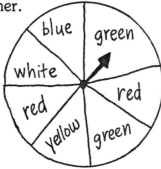

blue green
white
red red
yellow green

d) Wearing a blindfold, point to one day in February. Probability of 16th:

_____

FEBRUARY

S	M	T	W	Th	F	S
1	2	3	4	5	6	7
8	9	10	11	12	13	14
15	16	17	18	19	20	21
22	23	24	25	26	27	28

Student Page

Answers on page 240.

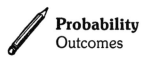

e) Drop a dime on the floor.
Probability of tails: _____

f) Roll a die. Probability of rolling a 4: _____

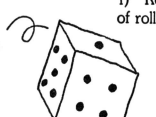

g) Spin the spinner. Probability of landing on C:
_____

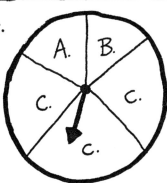

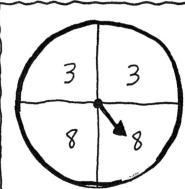

h) Spin the spinner. Probability of landing on 3:
_____

i) Wearing a blind-fold, draw one name from the hat. Probability of drawing Rob:
_____

j) Randomly choose a record. Probability of choosing jazz: _____

ROCK CLASSICAL POP COUNTRY

k) Wearing a blindfold, choose a candy. Probability of choosing a lollipop:
_____

l) Wearing a blind-fold, choose an ice cream cone. Probability of choosing vanilla:
_____

Probability
Outcomes

PUTTING ON SOCKS IN THE DARK

Preparation:

- Have students bring socks of various colors to class.
- Have a box or bucket and a blindfold for each group of five students. In each container put several socks (5-8). Be sure to include three or more different colors.

Use:

1) Explain probability to the class. Show them how to write a fraction showing the probability of an event occurring.
2) Divide students into small groups. Give each group a container of socks. Have the students make charts similar to the one below in order to keep track of the outcomes of drawing socks from the box. The colors students write will, of course, depend on the colors of socks they have.
3) First, students should note the probability of drawing each color. Then, have each student (blindfolded) draw a sock five times. The group should keep track of the outcomes.
4) Compare the outcome chart to the fractions which students wrote for probability.

How Many Socks In Total? _____

PICK	COLOR	HOW MANY SOCKS THAT COLOR?	PROBABILITY
1st Pick			
2nd Pick			
3rd Pick			
4th Pick			
5th Pick			

Teacher Page

Name _____

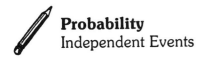

THROWING MONEY AROUND

If you throw a quarter and a dime on the floor, what is the probability that both will land "heads up"?

The way each coin falls has no effect on the other coin. Thus, the events that occur are said to be independent.

Usually, if two events are independent, the probability that both will occur is the product of their individual probabilities.

The probability of the quarter landing "heads up" is one out of two.

$$\frac{1}{2} \times \frac{1}{2} = \frac{1}{4}$$

The probability of the dime landing "heads up" is one out of two.

The probability of both landing "heads up" is one out of four.

Toss two coins 20 times. Keep track of the outcomes on this chart. How many times did both coins land "heads up"?

COIN #1	TALLY	COIN #2	TALLY
H		H	
H		T	
T		H	
T		T	

Student Page

GET YOUR SCHOOL POPPIN'

Preparation:
- You'll need lots of popcorn, popcorn poppers, a supply of paper bags and a scale for weighing the popped corn.
- Inform the teachers in your school that you'd like to do a math activity in your room which will involve other classes. Ask them to let you know if they're willing to participate in a popcorn eating experiment.

Use:
1) Tell students that they will be making graphs which show how much popcorn each grade in your school can eat. Discuss your plans for gathering the data necessary for making such graphs.

   Consider:
   how you will make the popcorn
   how you will weigh and distribute it
   how you will inform the other classes about the "test"
   how you will keep track of what has been eaten in each class

2) Gather the statistics and agree on a format for the graph. Graphs need not be exactly alike, but each must be a pictograph having a title and a key to explain any symbols used. All graphs should accurately convey the data.

3) Don't forget to include yourselves in the experiment! Also, you might like to discover how much popcorn the school administrators and other personnel can eat.

Teacher Page

160

Name _____

WHAT DOES "MEAN" MEAN?

Mean is the average of all the given data. To find the mean, divide the sum of the items by the number of items.

Median is found by arranging all items in order from least to greatest and determining which one falls in the middle.

Range is the difference between the greatest number and the smallest number.

Mode is the item or items that appear most frequently.

Snow Records At Ski Resorts

Snowpass..................102
Big Bird Mountain.......87
White Bear Valley........122
The Sixth Mountain......134
Winter Pass..............98
SnowPark................98
Powderhorn..............115

For the data above, find the:

1. mean _____

2. mode _____

3. median _____

4. range _____

Answers on page 240.

Student Page

BODY STATISTICS

Preparation:
- Make a copy of the student page "Pulse Patrol" for each student.
- You will need at least one stopwatch.

Use:
1) Teach students how to take a pulse. Have each student lay three fingers of his or her right hand on the left side of the neck beside the adam's apple (on the carotid artery) and press lightly to feel a heartbeat.
2) When everyone has been sitting quietly for at least 10 minutes, have them take a resting heart rate. Have students count their heartbeats for 15 seconds and then multiply the number of beats by 4.
3) Take students outdoors or to the gym and have them walk briskly for five minutes. Have each student count his or her pulse for 10 seconds and then multiply the number of beats by 6.
4) Have students walk slowly again for five minutes. Let them take their recovery pulses by counting their heartbeats for 15 seconds and then multiplying the number of beats by 4.
5) Use the following student page for recording heart rate data and for helping make individual line graphs using their data.

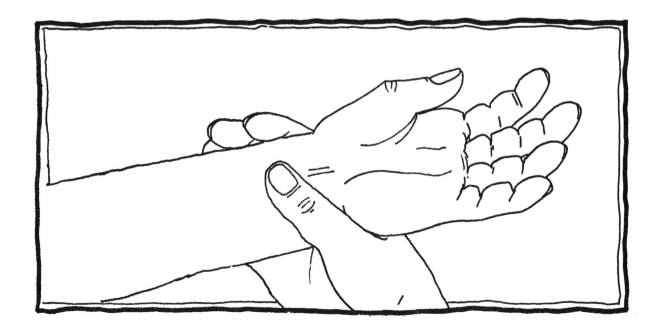

Statistics
Gathering Data
Line Graphs

Name ______________________________

PULSE PATROL

Data CHART	BEATS PER MINUTE
RESTING PULSE	
AFTER 5 min.	
AFTER 10 min.	
AFTER 15 min.	
AFTER 20 min. (recovery pulse)	

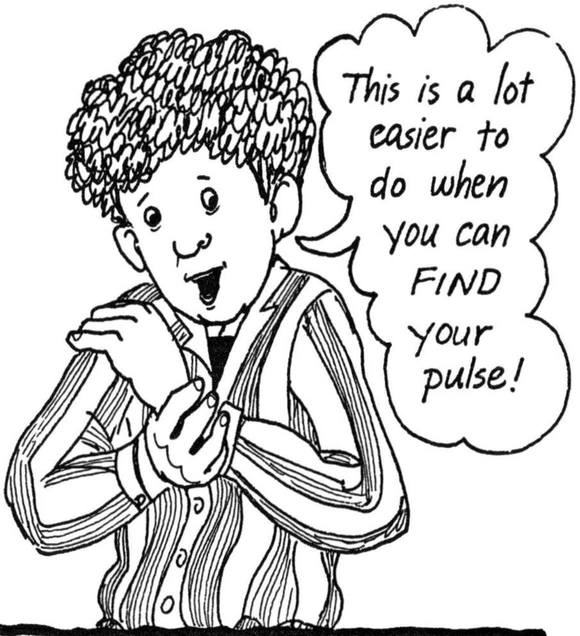

This is a lot easier to do when you can FIND your pulse!

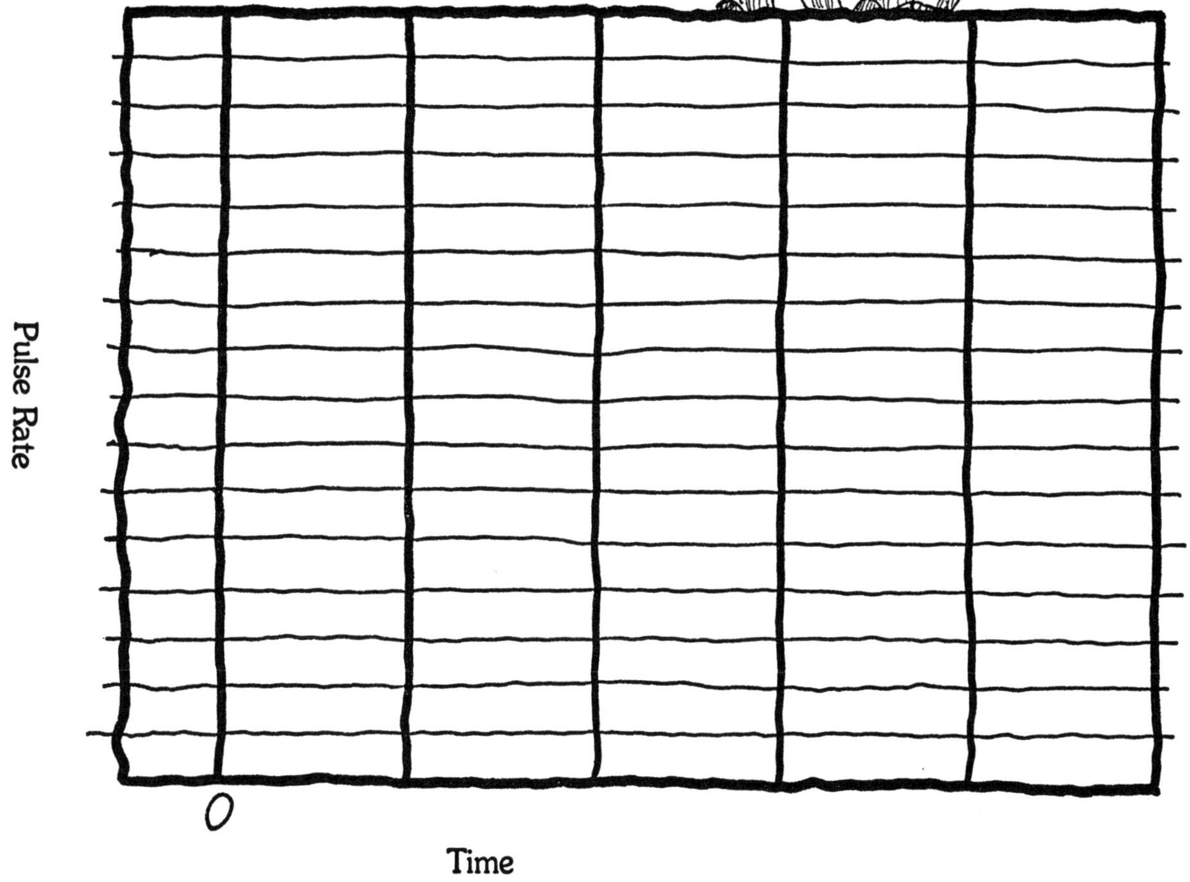

Pulse Rate
0
Time

Student Page

Graphing
Circle Graphs

A GOOD USE OF TIME

Preparation:
- Cut enough poster board circles (16 inch diameter or larger) for your class.
- Have colored construction paper, markers and rulers available for students to use.

Use:
1) Talk with students about the ways they use their time during an average school day.
2) Agree on categories of time use (school, sleep, study, T.V., exercise, lessons, visiting friends, etc.). The categories may vary from one individual to the next.
3) Show students an example of a circle graph (perhaps one you've done showing how you use your time), and discuss methods for dividing a circle accurately.
4) Have each student make a chart of time use and transfer that data to the circle in a circle graph form.

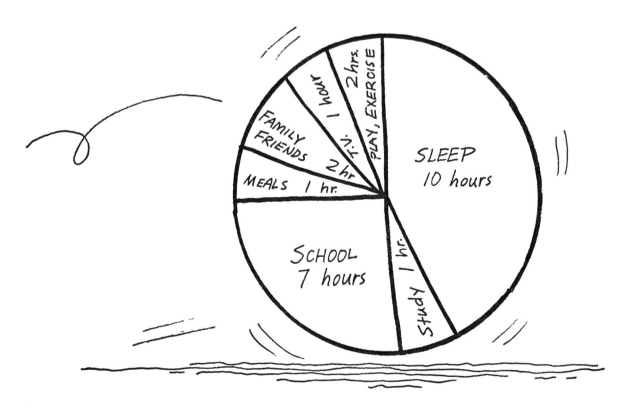

OF WEREWOLVES

AND ZOMBIES

WEREWOLF - ZOMBIE SIGHTINGS 1880-1889

WERE WOLVES

ZOMBIES

WEREWOLVES ARE SCARY!

The graph above shows the sightings of werewolves and zombies in Dracula Park over a period of 10 years. Use the information to answer these questions.

1) In what year did the sharpest drop in werewolf sightings occur? _____

2) What year had the largest number of combined sightings? _____

3) What year had the greatest increase in zombie sightings? _____

4) During these 10 years, were there more zombie or werewolf sightings? _____

5) In what year was there the greatest difference in the number of werewolf sightings and the number of zombie sightings? _____

Answers on page 240.

Student Page

Name _____

PIZZA POSSIBILITIES

Take your own pizza survey and show the results on the bar graph below. Ask 40 people this question: "What would be your first choice for a pizza topping (other than cheese) and what would be your last choice?"

Make 1st choice bar 1 color, last choice bar 2nd color.

Toppings	First Choice	Last Choice
PEPPERONI		
SAUSAGE		
BEEF		
SALAMI		
MUSHROOMS		
OLIVES		
ONIONS		
PINEAPPLE		
ANCHOVIES		
OTHER		

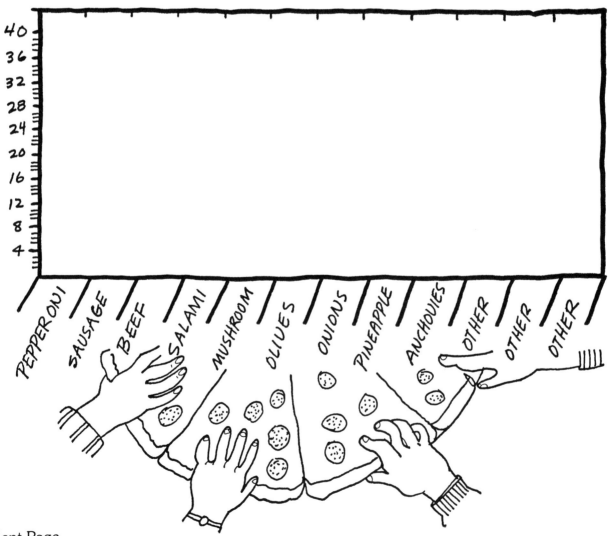

Student Page

166

PRE-ALGEBRA

Preparation:

- Prepare a list of equation statements such as the examples below.

Use:

1) Ask students to number 1-10 on paper and listen to each expression as you dictate. After evaluating the expression, each student should write T or F to tell if the expression is a true equation or if it is not an equation (false).

2) Dictate expressions such as:

- For $10 = y - 7$ . . . y is 3
- For $25\,m = 125$ . . . m is 15
- For $49 = z - 12$ . . . z is 60
- For $3(x + 7) = 33$ . . . x is 4
- For $x - 7 + y = 15$ . . . if y is 3, then x is 25
- For $190 = x + 2x$ . . . x = 65
- For $y = 19 - 2 + 7$ . . . y = 25
- For $256 = Z^2$ . . . .Z = 4
- For $4\,n = 414$ . . . n = 103.5

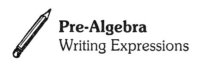
MATCHING PAIRS

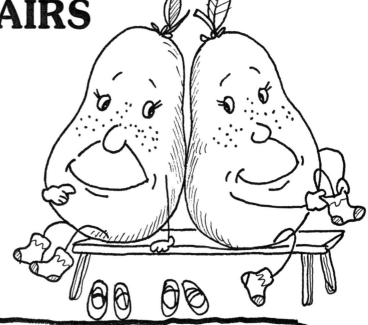

Write the letter of the correct mathematical expression in each blank. (There will be two letters remaining.)

_____ 1. five pounds less than John

_____ 2. twelve more than a number

_____ 3. ten less than a number

_____ 4. Janice ran seven times farther

_____ 5. fifty times the price less seven

_____ 6. two more than the difference between
ninety and another number

_____ 7. ten times the cost

_____ 8. twice the sum of two numbers

_____ 9. the quotient of 8 and another number

_____ 10. twice the sum of n, plus 5

_____ 11. four times the quotient of 5 and x

_____ 12. twice x divided by 7

A. $\frac{8}{y}$

B. $2n + 5$

C. $4\left(\frac{5}{x}\right)$

D. $2x + y$

E. $7n$

F. $z - 10$

G. $m - 5$

H. $2(n + 5)$

I. $10y$

J. $50a - 7$

K. $\frac{2x}{7}$

L. $12 + x$

M. $2(x + y)$

N. $90 - c + 2$

WHICH HAT?

On each rabbit there is a simplified expression found in expanded form on one of the hats.
Match each rabbit with the hat out of which it came.

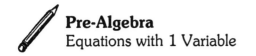

Name _____

MISSING!

Help the bloodhound follow the trail of the missing person by solving the equation in each footstep.

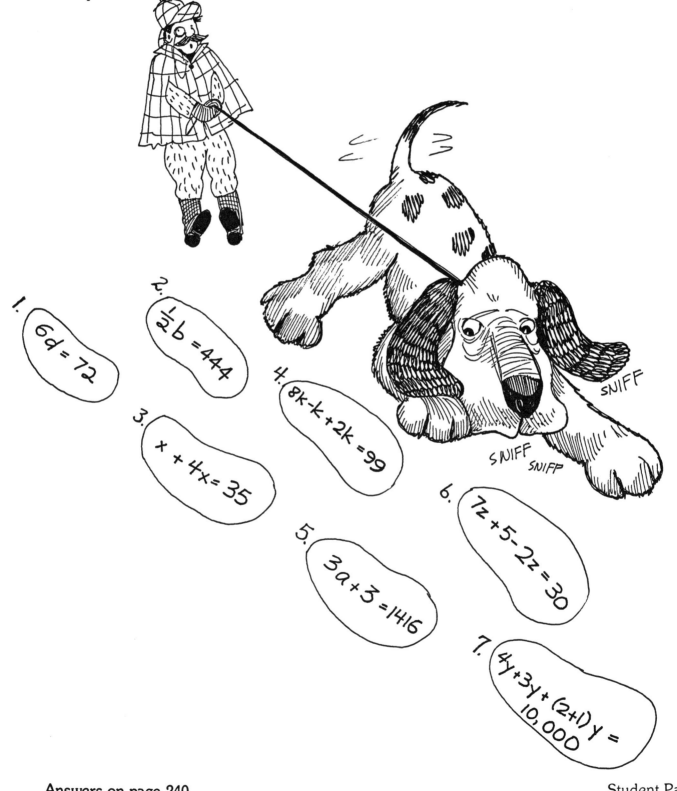

1. $6d = 72$

2. $\frac{1}{2}b = 444$

3. $x + 4x = 35$

4. $8k - k + 2k = 99$

5. $3a + 3 = 1416$

6. $7z + 5 - 2z = 30$

7. $4y + 3y + (2 + 1)y = 10,000$

SNIFF

SNIFF SNIFF

Name _____

I'VE GOT WHEELS!

Which "wheels" would you like? _____

What's the original cost (OC)? _____ Down payment (DP)? _____

Monthly installment payment (MIP)? _____

The total cost (TC)? _____

How much interest (I) will you pay altogether? _____

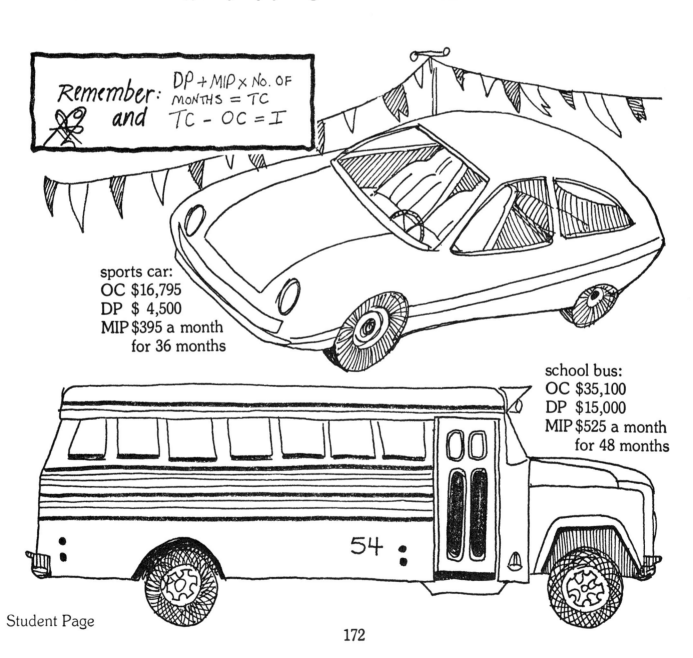

Remember: ~~X~~ and $DP + MIP \times$ No. of months $= TC$
$TC - OC = I$

sports car:
OC $16,795
DP $ 4,500
MIP $395 a month
for 36 months

school bus:
OC $35,100
DP $15,000
MIP $525 a month
for 48 months

54

Name _____

Smiley's
USED CARS

pickup
OC $4825
DP $1000
MIP $182.50 a month
for 24 months

old jeep
OC $3990
DP $1200
MIP $166.40 a month
for 24 months

collector's model
OC $55,569   DP $14,700 MIP $835.30 a month for 60 months

Recreational Vehicle
OC $18,229
DP $ 5,500
MIP $ 330.50 a month
for 48 months

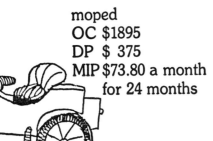

moped
OC $1895
DP $ 375
MIP $73.80 a month
for 24 months

Model T truck
OC $2865
DP $ 630
MIP $197 a month
for 12 months

How much interest would you save if you chose the
moped instead of the RV? _____

INTEGER INVESTIGATIONS

Preparation:

- Make copies of the student page "Fooling Around With Integers" for your class.

Use:

1) Review with students the processes for the four basic operations with positive and negative integers. Use the student page "Fooling Around With Integers" to practice these processes.

2) After doing a few sample problems together, dictate the following problems to students so they can try some on their own. There is space for them to write and solve the equations on the student page.

1)	$144 \div -12$	5)	$-180 \div -60$
2)	$47 + (-77)$	6)	-81×-20
3)	$-99 + 70$	7)	-30×11
4)	$-52 - (-40)$	8)	1000×-77

Name _____

FOOLING AROUND WITH INTEGERS

It helps to know the rules when using integers to solve problems. Here they are:

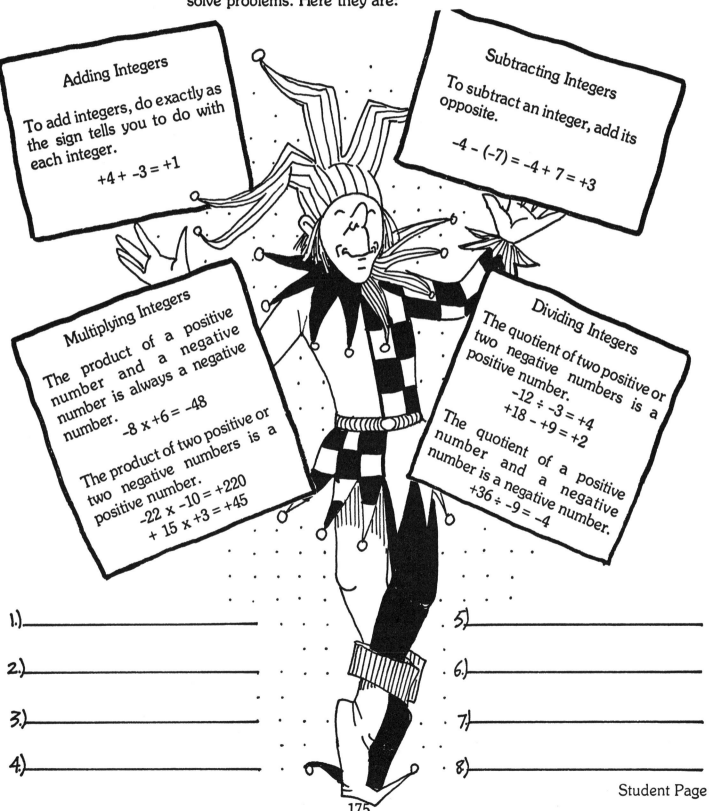

Adding Integers

To add integers, do exactly as the sign tells you to do with each integer.

$$+4 + -3 = +1$$

Subtracting Integers

To subtract an integer, add its opposite.

$$-4 - (-7) = -4 + 7 = +3$$

Multiplying Integers

The product of a positive number and a negative number is always a negative number.

$$-8 \times +6 = -48$$

The product of two positive or two negative numbers is a positive number.

$$-22 \times -10 = +220$$
$$+ 15 \times +3 = +45$$

Dividing Integers

The quotient of two positive or two negative numbers is a positive number.

$$-12 \div -3 = +4$$
$$+18 - +9 = +2$$

The quotient of a positive number and a negative number is a negative number.

$$+36 \div -9 = -4$$

1.) _____

2.) _____

3.) _____

4.) _____

5.) _____

6.) _____

7.) _____

8.) _____

Student Page

175

Name _____

DATE DETECTIVES

You can solve the following mysteries using this secret formula. Here's how it works:

$$\text{Total} = d + 2m + \frac{3m + 3}{5} + y + \frac{y}{4} - \frac{y}{100} + \frac{y}{400} + 2$$

d = day of the month, using numbers 1-31

m = month, March is 3, April is 4, May is 5, and so on (except January is 13 and February is 14)

y = year -- except for January and February dates, when you use the *previous* year

(When you do the divisions, use only the whole numbers of quotients and ignore the remainders.)

Take the total and divide it by 7. Look at the remainder.

0 = Saturday, 1 = Sunday, 2 = Monday, 3 = Tuesday,
4 = Wednesday, 5 = Thursday, 6 = Friday

Mystery A

On what day of the week did Christmas fall in 1983?

$$T = 25 + 2(12) + \frac{3(12) + 3}{5} + 1983 + \frac{1983}{4} - \frac{1983}{100} + \frac{1983}{400} + 2$$

T = 25 + 24 + 7 + 1983 + 495 – 19 + 4 + 2

T = 2521

$$7\overline{)2521} \quad 360 \text{ r } 1$$

Christmas fell on Sunday in 1983.

Mystery # 1

On what day of the week were you born?

Mystery # 2

What day of the week will Valentine's Day be three years from now?

Mystery # 3

On what day will it be the first day of the year 2000?

Mystery # 4

What day of the week was July 4, 1776?

Mystery # 5

Does this formula work for today's date? Find out.

Mystery # 6

What day of the week will it be when you turn 18?

Mystery # 7

What day of the week will the next leap year day fall on?

Mystery # 8

Will March 13, 2013 be Friday the 13th?

* Because of the change in the calendar on September 14, 1752, days before this date will not follow this formula.

Student Page

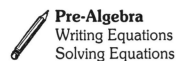

Pre-Algebra
Writing Equations
Solving Equations

Name _____

HOW OLD IS TOM?

Jamie   Katy   Tom   Mandy   Jenny   Ramon

1. Jamie is four times as old as Tom.
   The difference between their ages is eight years less than the sum of their ages.

   How old is Tom? _____   Jamie? _____

2. Mandy is now twice Katy's age. In six years she will be 1½ times Katy's age.

   How old is Katy? _____   Mandy? _____

3. Ramon is six times Jenny's age. In 12 years he'll only be twice her age.

   How old is Ramon? _____   Jenny? _____

PROBLEM SOLVING

SCUBA LOGIC

Scooby Dooby Dan, Frannie Fin, and Gayle Goggles took scuba diving trips for very particular reasons. One was tracking a shark, one was searching for treasure on sunken ships, and one was exploring the great reef.

Only one of the following four statements is true.

Find out who was diving for what. First write all of the possibilities (there are six). Then test each possibility against the statements. Work for 15 minutes or more before asking the teacher for a clue (found on page 240 of this book).

1. Frannie Fin was diving for treasure.
2. Scooby Dooby Dan did NOT go to the reef.
3. Scooby Dooby Dan was not tracking the shark.
4. Frannie Fin was NOT tracking the shark.

Scooby Dan

Gayle Goggles

Frannie Fin

Problem Solving
Varied Operations

Name _____

IN THE SPORTS ARENA

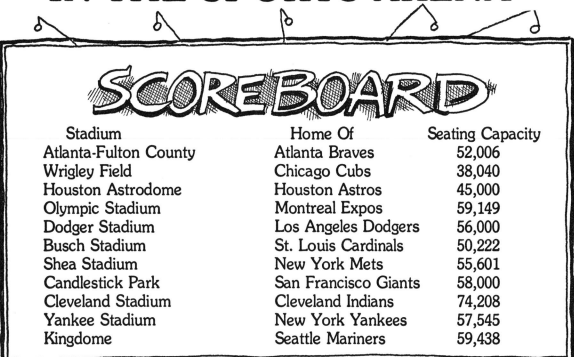

Stadium	Home Of	Seating Capacity
Atlanta-Fulton County	Atlanta Braves	52,006
Wrigley Field	Chicago Cubs	38,040
Houston Astrodome	Houston Astros	45,000
Olympic Stadium	Montreal Expos	59,149
Dodger Stadium	Los Angeles Dodgers	56,000
Busch Stadium	St. Louis Cardinals	50,222
Shea Stadium	New York Mets	55,601
Candlestick Park	San Francisco Giants	58,000
Cleveland Stadium	Cleveland Indians	74,208
Yankee Stadium	New York Yankees	57,545
Kingdome	Seattle Mariners	59,438

1. What is the average number of seats in all of the arenas? _____

2. Forty-two thousand fans are watching the Dodgers play at home. What percentage of the seats are empty? _____

3. Kingdome holds _____ more people than Wrigley Field. _____

4. If Yankee Stadium is 75% full, how many fans are present? _____

5. If 58% of a full house at the Atlanta-Fulton County Stadium have bought a hot dog, how many hot dogs have been sold? _____

6. Candlestick Park is 90% full. If an average of 1/2 lb. of popcorn is eaten per fan, how much popcorn will be eaten? _____

7. A 62% capacity crowd is watching the Expos and a 58% capacity crowd is watching the Indians. Which stadium has more people? _____

8. How many more people are watching the Mets than the Cardinals on a day when both stadiums are full? _____

Answers on page 240.

Student Page

Problem Solving
Statistics

CHOCOLATE CHIP SEARCH

Preparation:
- Gather all necessary ingredients and supplies for making chocolate chip cookies (use a recipe of your choice).
- Collect measuring tools for determining linear size and weight.

Use:
1) Have the class work together to make chocolate chip cookies. Allow students to follow the recipe and bake the cookies in a school oven, if possible.
2) Use the cookies for calculating statistics and for solving problems. Begin by having students complete the student page "Cookie Calculations." Each student will need one or two cookies in order to complete the calculations. After students have completed their student pages, allow the class to eat the remaining cookies!

Are we good — or what !?!

COOKIE CALCULATIONS

Before eating a cookie, find out:

_____ its weight in grams

_____ the area of one surface

_____ its approximate volume

_____ the diameter

_____ the perimeter

_____ the number of chips in the cookie (estimation)

As you eat the cookie, find out:

_____ the number of chews per bite

_____ the weight of one chip in grams

_____ the number of bites required to eat one cookie

As a class, determine:

_____ the average number of chips
per cookie in all of the cookies
eaten by your class

_____ the total number of chocolate chips
eaten by the class (estimation)

Student Page

183

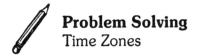

Name _____

A MATTER OF TIME

Use the information on the time zone map (next page) to solve the problems below. You will also need a world map or a globe to help you find these places.

Ramon lives in
   Tegucigalpa, Honduras.
Sonja lives in Moscow, U.S.S.R.
Thomas lives in Sydney, Australia.
Sara lives in
   San Francisco, California.
Me Ling lives in Peking, China.
Usha lives in Bombay, India.
Eduardo lives in
   New York City, New York.
Caroline lives in London, England.
Maria lives in Rio de Janeiro, Brazil.
It is now 9 a.m. in Rio de Janeiro
   and Maria is in school.

1. Who is having supper now? _____ (time: _____)

2. Which two persons are probably _____ (time: _____)

   asleep now? _____ (time: _____)

3. Who is just getting out of bed? _____ (time: _____)

4. Who is on their way home from school? _____ (time: _____)

5. Who is eating breakfast? _____ (time: _____)

6. Who is getting ready for bed? _____ (time: _____)

7. Who is eating lunch? _____ (time: _____)

8. What would you be doing right now? _____ (time: _____)

Student Page

Answers on page 240.

Name _____

TIME ZONE MAP

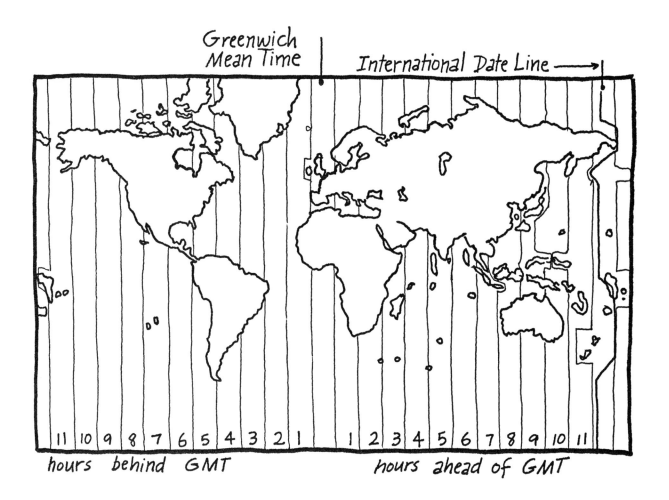

The world is divided into 24 time zones. When traveling, one must change the time on his or her watch whenever entering a new time zone.

The zones are measured east and west of Greenwich, England. The time in Greenwich is called Greenwich Mean Time.

When traveling east of Greenwich, you add an hour for each time zone. When traveling west of Greenwich, you subtract an hour for each time zone.

By the time you reach the other side of the world, you have gained or lost one day. This point is the International Date Line.

Student Page

FAMILY TREE TALLIES

Preparation:
- Make copies of the student page "How Many Cousins?" for your students.
- Gather large sheets of drawing paper, crayons and markers for making family trees.

Use:
1) Let students enjoy solving Chester's dilemma on the student page.
2) Give students time to make lists of their relatives. (They may need a few days to track down family information.)
3) Discuss ideas for creating family trees that contain the names of all of the living relatives. (Extended and combined families will require special planning.) Let students create their own family trees.
4) When the students have completed their trees, ask each student to write four questions related to his or her family statistics. Students may trade family trees and answer one another's questions.

Name _____

HOW MANY COUSINS?

Meet Chester and several of his relatives. Chester is trying to figure out just how many relatives he has. Help him!

Chester's mother has three married sisters (one with three children, two with two children each) and two married brothers (one with one child, one with four children).

Chester's father has three brothers. Two brothers are married and have two children each. The other brother is single.

Chester has four grandparents. Chester has one sister and one brother.

1) How many cousins does Chester have? _____
2) How many aunts does Chester have? _____ How many uncles? _____
3) How many grandchildren do Chester's mother's parents have? _____
4) How many grandchildren do Chester's father's parents have? _____
5) How many people would there be at a family reunion with everyone there? _____

Answers on page 240.

Student Page

187

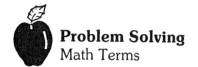

I WANT TO BE IN PICTURES

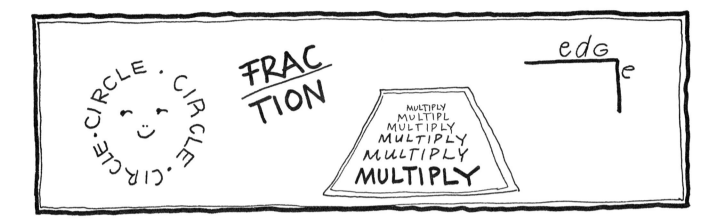

Preparation:
- Draw two or three of the examples below on posters or the chalkboard.

Use:
1) Show students the examples of math terms written in a way that shows or explains the meanings.
2) Ask students to think of other terms that may be written in "picture form."
3) Provide poster board or drawing paper for students to make picture definitions of math terms. (Refer students to the glossary in this book if necessary.)
4) Use the finished pictures for a bulletin board display. Students may add written definitions to accompany the pictured math terms.

Problem Solving
Varied Operations

Name _____

ROLLER COASTER CALCULATIONS

1) There are nine cars in a particular roller coaster. Each car has two sections. Each section holds two people. How many people will the roller coaster hold? _____

2) If 18 people are in the roller coaster, what percentage of the seats are full? _____

3) The roller coaster travels 2.4 miles in 3.6 minutes. How many miles does it travel per minute? _____

4) The roller coaster ride has four separate trains. Each train makes seven trips an hour. The park is open from 10 a.m. to midnight. How many trips do all of the trains make in one day? _____

5) If all of the cars in every train are full on every trip, how many people could ride in one day? _____

6) Approximately 14 people a day "chicken out" before getting on the roller coaster. If the park is open all but two weeks a year, how many people "chicken out" each year? _____

7) John has been to this park three times a year since he was six years old. Now he's 15. Each time he visits the park he takes five rides on the roller coaster. How many rides has he taken during his life? _____

PASSING ZONE

Preparation:
- You will need brown construction paper, scissors, markers and tape.
- Have several students make a large cut-out figure of a football player ready to pass a ball.

Use:
1) Display the football player cutout on a bulletin board or tape it on the chalkboard.
2) Talk about what a completion record means to a passer on a football team. (A percentage found by comparing the number of successfully completed passes to the number attempted.) Students may wish to use reference materials to find completion records of well-known players.
3) Have each student make a construction paper football. Each student should write a hypothetical number of attempted passes and a hypothetical number of completed passes on the football.
4) Put an identifying number or letter on each ball and tape the balls around the room so that they can be seen. Students must find the completion percentage for each football problem.

QUARTERBACK'S QUANDRY

How smart is Quarterback Quincy Ironarm? For each play he must decide which player should be the pass receiver. Help him out by following the clues to find the correct player's number.

Play 1
225,500 hot dogs have been eaten by 20,500 fans. The average number of hot dogs eaten by each fan is the correct player's number.

Player # _____

Play 2
The number of teams that play in a game multiplied by the number of legs on the field at one time is the correct player's number.

Player # _____

Play 3
The total number of injuries of seven players with taped knees, nine players with taped backs, and three players with taped ankles is the correct player's number.

Player # _____

Play 4
Each of three referees blows a whistle 29 times per quarter. The total number of whistles per quarter is the correct player's number.

Player # _____

Play 5
Eighteen cheerleaders multiplied by seven handstands, minus the number of goal posts on a field, minus the yards in a football field, plus the quarterback's number equals the correct player's number.

Player # _____

Answers on page 240.

Student Page

191

WHITHER THE WEATHER?

STATISTICS

normal high temp (by month)
normal low temp (by month)
record high temperature
record low temperature
average annual precipitation
average annual rainfall
average annual snowfall
average number of sunny days (by month)
average number of cloudy days (by month)
fastest wind recorded
average relative humidity (by month)

Preparation:
- Gather area or state weather statistics from local news agencies or the weather bureau. (Involve students in this, if possible.)
- Have poster board, measuring sticks, and markers available.

Use:
1) Let students work in groups to transfer the accumulated weather information on charts in clear, readable writing. Added illustrations make the charts more interesting.
2) Post the charts in places where students can see them and get to them easily.
3) Ask students to use the weather information to create five to ten math problems for classmates. Encourage students to include a variety of operations.
4) Compile all of the problems to make a weather station in the classroom where each student may go and choose ten math problems to solve.

what a great day!

Teacher Page

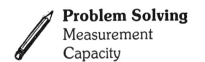

SEE YOU ON THE TRAIL

Andrea and Jay are packing their backpacks for a hike to Redstone Ridge. How much stuff can they fit in their backpacks? Help them pack!

Notice the volume capacity of each pack and the volume of each item. Next to each backpack, list as many of the items that will fit into it. What will you choose to leave behind?

Student Page

193

GETTING RID OF THE EXTRAS

For each example below, one piece of information is not helpful in solving the problem. Cross out this unnecessary information and then solve the problem.

① The toboggan run is 2600 yards long. This toboggan averages about 30 yards per second. The total weight of the tobogganers is 236 pounds. How long will it take to complete the run?

② James can wash 210 plates an hour. He worked three hours on Saturday, five hours on Sunday, and two hours on Monday. How long does it take him to wash each plate?

③ Hot Rod Renee needs a 15% down payment for a car. The cost of the car is $6995. The monthly payments are $137. How much money does she need for the down payment?

④ Kurt and Jason are loading skateboards onto a truck that has a 140 cubic foot capacity. The truck holds 1/2 ton. Each skateboard takes up 840 cubic inches. How many skateboards will fit in the truck?

⑤ Sally has seven blue socks and three white socks in a drawer. She picks out two socks without looking. The drawer measures 8" x 22" x 13". What is the probability that both socks will be blue?

Problem Solving
Logic

Name _____

WILL THE REAL AGENT 008 PLEASE STAND UP?

You have been assigned to give a secret message to agent 008, but four agents claim to be 008.

Use the clues below to find out each agent's hangout and mission. In doing this you will also discover which agent is really agent 008!

Missions:
- to find an electronic brain which was stolen by a villain
- to discover submarine secrets
- to recapture a top secret formula for chocolate ice cream
- to capture a jewel thief

Code Names:
Neon
King Kong
Rocky Road
Santa Claus

Hangouts:
Hideaway Hotel
Wally's Waterbed Warehouse
Sleuth's Sandwich Shop
Snoop University

Clues:
1. Neon does not hang out at the Hideaway Hotel.
2. The agent who frequents Sleuth's Sandwich Shop is trying to capture the jewel thief.
3. Rocky Road wears the disguise of a student.
4. King Kong is looking for submarine secrets.
5. Neon is not looking for a top secret formula for chocolate ice cream.
6. The agent searching for the electronic brain is often seen at Snoop University.
7. Santa Claus hates waterbeds.
8. The real agent 008 is searching for the electronic brain.

Answers on page 240.

ONCE UPON A MASQUERADE

Discover what number is hiding behind each costumed character by solving the problems below.

A) The sum of my digits equals 11. The ones digit minus the hundreds digit equals 3. No digit is less than 2.

B) I am 6^8.

C) Add me to 200 and you will get a palindrome. Subtract me from 875 and you will get 348.

D) Multiply my number by itself and you will get 400 *centuries*.

Student Page

Answers on page 240.

Name _____

E) I'm less than 10 multiplied by 500. I'm more than 12,000 divided by 40. I'm more than 8285 minus 4556. I'm less than 8^4 and I have three sevens.

F) I equal 59 dozen minus 4 score.

G) I am the number of days in 2/3 of 12 leap years.

H) The name of my number tells how many letters are in my name.

Answers on page 240.

197

Student Page

WILL YOU DINE WITH ME?

Use the menu from the Zooside Deli and the given orders (next page) to answer the questions below.

1) Agatha Ape took Stephen Spider to brunch. What was their total bill with 5% tax and a 12% tip?
2) Paul Peacock is a generous tipper. He left a 22% tip. How much did he leave for a tip?
3) Did Georgia Giraffe pay more or less for lunch than Tabatha Turtle and by how much (no tax)?
4) Georgia and Tabatha each left a 15% tip. What was the difference in their tips?
5) Samantha Shark, being a bit stingy, took the waiter's left arm and left only a 3% tip. The waiter, being a bit distracted, forgot to add the tax. What was the total amount Samantha paid?

Name _____

ZOOSIDE DELI MENU

Entrées
Fried Snail Claws.............$ 2.25
Pine Needle Salad...............$ 2.50
Fresh Seaweed...............$ 1.95
Broiled Inchworms...........$ 6.75
Minnow Minestrone Soup..............
    .95 per cup....$ 1.50 per bowl
Beetles Au Gratin.............$ 3.80
Sautéed Bark Strips........$10.90
Potato Bug Casserole.......$ 4.50
Maple Leaf Soufflé ....$ 6.75
Bar-B-Q Moss Burgers.......$ 3.50
Deep Fried Cod Tails...........$ 5.95
Birdseed Tofu Bake..........$ 4.80
        ½ portion...$ 3.00

Beverages
Iced Sea Water.............$ .75
Mud Puddle Shake...........$ 2.00
Algae Phosphate ....$ .80
Hot Rainwater Tea...........$ .50

AGATHA APE

Snail Claws
Maple Leaf Soufflé
Rainwater Tea

GEORGIA GIRAFFE

Sautéed Bark Strips
Maple Leaf Soufflé
Bar-B-Q Moss Burger
Algae Phosphate

PAUL PEACOCK

Inchworms
Beetles
Birdseed Tofu
  (½ portion)
Mud Puddle Shake

TABATHA TURTLE

3 orders of
Beetles
Mud Puddle Shake

STEPHEN SPIDER

Beetles
Potato Bug Casserole
Pine Needle Salad
Rainwater Tea

SAMANTHA SHARK

Fresh Seaweed
Cod Tails
    Minnow Soup
    Iced Sea Water

Student Page

STOP THE BOMB

DOWN

1. A side of a space figure.
3. A number whose factors are 1 and itself.
4. A property stating that the grouping of addends or factors does not affect the sum or product.
5. The factor by which you divide in division.
7. A drawing showing relationships of numbers.
9. A three-sided figure.

ACROSS

2. A figure with six equal sides.
4. A number being added.
6. A parallelogram with congruent sides.
8. To divide into two congruent parts.
10. A numeral placed at the top right of a numeral which tells how many times the number is to be multiplied by itself.
11. Any member of the set of positive or negative numbers.
12. The measure of capacity.

The fuse on this bomb takes 20 minutes to burn. You have 20 minutes to solve the puzzle and stop the fuse. Can you do it? Mark off $\frac{1}{4}$ of the fuse every five minutes.

MATH TOOLS & TREASURES

MATH SKILLS FOR MIDDLE GRADES

Numeration and Number Concepts

- ____ Associating word names with corresponding numerals
- ____ Reading and writing numerals with 1 to 12 or more digits
- ____ Identifying place value to the billions
- ____ Expressing numerals in expanded notation
- ____ Devising an original numeration system
- ____ Identifying the value of all U.S. coins and bills
- ____ Reading and writing Roman numerals
- ____ Distinguishing between numerals having the same digits in different positions
- ____ Reading and writing numerals for fractional numbers
- ____ Reading and writing mixed fractional numbers
- ____ Reading and writing decimal numerals
- ____ Reading and writing mixed decimal numerals
- ____ Expressing fractional numerals in expanded notation
- ____ Expressing decimal numerals in expanded notation
- ____ Reading and writing positive and negative integers
- ____ Reading and writing exponential numbers
- ____ Reading and writing percentages
- ____ Comparing and sequencing whole numbers
- ____ Comparing and sequencing fractional numbers
- ____ Comparing and sequencing decimal numbers
- ____ Comparing and sequencing integers
- ____ Reading and writing sentences using the symbols $\langle$ and $\rangle$
- ____ Identifying odd and even numbers
- ____ Identifying prime and composite numbers
- ____ Understanding the value and properties of zero
- ____ Rounding whole numbers
- ____ Rounding fractions
- ____ Rounding decimals
- ____ Finding the intersection and union of two sets
- ____ Forming Cartesian sets
- ____ Using Venn Diagrams to represent sets

Operations With Whole Numbers

- ____ Learning sums through 20
- ____ Learning differences through 20
- ____ Recognizing the inverse relationship between addition and subtraction
- ____ Using the terms addend, difference, and sum
- ____ Recognizing zero as the identity element for addition
- ____ Using the commutative property for addition
- ____ Using the associative property for addition
- ____ Finding the missing addend in number sentences
- ____ Adding long columns
- ____ Renaming places up to millions
- ____ Estimating sums and differences
- ____ Adding and subtracting numbers with up to 12 digits
- ____ Seeing multiplication as the joining of equivalent sets
- ____ Seeing multiplication as repeated addition
- ____ Seeing division as separation of sets into equivalent subsets
- ____ Seeing division as repeated subtraction

_____ Recognizing the inverse relationship between multiplication & division
_____ Learning multiplication & division facts using factors through 20
_____ Using the terms factor, product, quotient, divisor, & remainder
_____ Identifying the factors of a whole number
_____ Identifying common factors of whole numbers
_____ Identifying the greatest common factor of two or more whole numbers
_____ Giving the multiples of a whole number
_____ Identifying common multiples of whole numbers
_____ Identifying the least common multiple of two or more whole numbers
_____ Supplying missing factors in multiplication and division problems
_____ Discovering the role of zero in multiplication & division
_____ Identifying 1 as the identity element in multiplication or division
_____ Using the associative property for multiplication
_____ Multiplying & dividing by 10 & multiples of 10
_____ Estimating products & quotients
_____ Multiplying several digits by 1,2,3,4, & 5-digit numerals
_____ Dividing several digits by 1,2,3,4, & 5-digit divisors
_____ Checking division problems using multiplication
_____ Checking multiplication by casting out 9s
_____ Finding averages
_____ Determining if whole numbers are divisible by 2,3,4,5,6,9,10

Fractions and Decimals

_____ Identifying fractional parts
_____ Using fractions to name parts of sets
_____ Identifying the numerator and denominator of fractions
_____ Identifying like fractions
_____ Adding and subtracting like fractions
_____ Identifying equivalent fractions
_____ Finding the greatest common factor for the numerator and denominator of
          a fraction
_____ Identifying non-equivalent fractions
_____ Identifying improper fractions
_____ Identifying mixed numerals
_____ Expressing fractions in lowest terms
_____ Expressing improper fractions as mixed numerals
_____ Expressing mixed numerals as improper fractions
_____ Finding the least common multiple for the denominators of two or more fractions
_____ Expressing fractions as like fractions
_____ Adding and subtracting unlike fractions
_____ Adding and subtracting mixed numerals
_____ Multiplying fractions
_____ Multiplying & dividing mixed numerals
_____ Identifying the reciprocals of fractions
_____ Dividing fractions using the reciprocal method
_____ Ordering fractions
_____ Using dollar signs & decimal points to write money amounts
_____ Adding, subtracting, multiplying & dividing with money
_____ Writing decimals to the thousandth's place
_____ Ordering decimals
_____ Expressing fractions as decimals
_____ Expressing decimals as fractions
_____ Adding, subtracting, multiplying, & dividing decimals
_____ Identifying terminating & repeating decimals
_____ Estimating sums, differences, products, & dividends with decimals

Ratio, Proportion, and Percent
_____ Understanding the meaning of ratio, proportion, & percent
_____ Finding ratios
_____ Expressing ratios as fractions
_____ Expressing ratios as decimals
_____ Finding proportions
_____ Using cross-multiplication to find ratio
_____ Finding percentages
_____ Expressing ratios as percentages
_____ Using ratio to find equivalent fractions
_____ Using ratio to identify similarity
_____ Using percent to find discounts, commissions interest
_____ Finding percentage of change

Measurement
_____ Estimating measurements
_____ Comparing measurements
_____ Recognizing & using the following units: inch, foot, yard, mile, millimeter, centimeter, meter, kilometer
_____ Recognizing & using the following units: cup, pint, quart, gallon, liter
_____ Recognizing & using the following units: ounce, pound, ton, milligram, gram, kilogram, metric ton
_____ Measuring length using English and metric systems
_____ Measuring liquid capacity in both systems
_____ Measuring temperatures in Fahrenheit and Celsius
_____ Measuring weights using English and metric systems
_____ Finding perimeters of regular and irregular polygons
_____ Finding the radius, diameter, and circumference of a circle
_____ Finding the area of circles and polygons
_____ Finding the capacity of space figures
_____ Finding the surface area of space figures
_____ Adding, subtracting, multiplying, and dividing measurements
_____ Identifying units of time: seconds, minutes, hours, days, weeks, months, years, decades, centuries
_____ Using a calendar to identify, add, subtract, and count time
_____ Telling time on a clock to the minute
_____ Recognizing the world's time zones
_____ Finding distances on a map
_____ Using a map scale to measure and identify distances

Geometry
_____ Identifying circles, triangles, rectangles, quadrilaterals, parallelograms, trapezoids
_____ Identifying closed and open figures
_____ Identifying and naming line segments
_____ Constructing line segments
_____ Identifying the intersection of lines
_____ Identifying and constructing parallel lines
_____ Identifying and constructing perpendicular lines
_____ Identifying and naming angles: right, obtuse, acute, straight
_____ Identifying and defining corresponding angles, complementary angles, supplementary angles
_____ Constructing and measuring angles
_____ Recognizing properties of circles, parallelograms, triangles
_____ Identifying congruent shapes
_____ Identifying similar figures
_____ Identifying the parts of a circle: radius, diameter, center, arc, chord, tangent, circumference
_____ Using a compass to draw circles
_____ Constructing a bisector for an angle
_____ Constructing a bisector for a line segment

_____ Constructing equilateral triangles
_____ Constructing congruent triangles
_____ Identifying cubes, other rectangular prisms, triangular prisms, cones, cylinders, pyramids, & spheres
_____ Naming and counting the faces, vertices & edges of space figures
_____ Identifying and drawing symmetrical figures
_____ Recognizing and drawing the slide of figures
_____ Recognizing and drawing the turn of figures
_____ Recognizing and drawing the flip of figures

Probability, Statistics, and Graphing

_____ Determining odds "in favor"
_____ Determining odds "against"
_____ Using a ratio to express probability
_____ Recording occurrence of events on a table
_____ Recording data on a graph
_____ Making predictions
_____ Conducting probability experiments
_____ Making tree diagrams
_____ Determining probability for independent events
_____ Determining probability for dependent events
_____ Finding range and mean
_____ Determining median and mode
_____ Reading and making circle graphs
_____ Reading and making bar graphs
_____ Reading and making line graphs
_____ Reading and making pictographs
_____ Reading and making histograms
_____ Gathering and graphing statistics
_____ Graphing ordered pairs
_____ Graphing equations
_____ Locating points on a four-quadrant grid
_____ Graphing ordered pairs of integers
_____ Graphing solution sets to linear equations
_____ Locating positions on the earth's grid

Problem Solving

_____ Choosing correct information
_____ Eliminating unnecessary information
_____ Choosing the correct operation
_____ Solving multi-step problems
_____ Writing an equation to solve a problem
_____ Solving word problems using:

     _____ All operations with whole numbers   _____ Statistics
     _____ All operations with decimals   _____ Probability
     _____ All operations with fractions   _____ Logic
     _____ Rate, Time & Distance   _____ Time
     _____ Ratio   _____ Money
     _____ Percentage   _____ Measurement
     _____ Maps   _____ Geometry

Pre-Algebra

_____ Identifying variables   _____ Solving equations with two variables
_____ Writing equations   _____ Using algebraic terms
_____ Solving equations with one variable
_____ Using algebraic formulas for problem solving
_____ Writing and evaluating mathematical expressions

GET YOUR NUMBERS STRAIGHT

Even Numbers—numbers that are divisible by 2

Odd Numbers—numbers that are not even

Prime Number—a number whose only factors are 1 and itself

Composite Numbers—all numbers that are not prime

Whole Numbers—a member of the set of numbers (0,1,2,3,4,5...)

Fractional Number—a number that can be written in the form a/b with a and b being any numbers, with the exception that b cannot be 0

Mixed Fractional Number—a number that has a whole number part and a fractional number part

Decimal Number—a number written with a decimal point to express a fraction whose denominator is 10 or a multiple of 10

Mixed Decimal Number—a number that has a whole number part and a decimal number part

Integers—the set of whole numbers (... -3, -2, -1, 0, 1, 2, 3 ...)

Positive Integers—the numbers to the right of 0 on a number line

Negative Integers—the numbers to the left of 0 on a number line

Rational Number—a number that can be written as a ratio a/b where both a and b are integers and b is not zero (all integers and decimals that repeat or terminate)

Irrational Number—a number that cannot be written as a quotient of two integers (decimals that neither repeat nor terminate)

Real Numbers—rational and irrational numbers together are the set of real numbers

Opposite Numbers—two numbers that are the same distance from 0 but are on opposite sides of 0 (3 is the opposite of -3)

Exponential Numbers—a number with an exponent, an exponent being a number written next to and above a base number to show how many times the base is to be used as a factor

Digit—one number in a numeral that holds a particular place

Significant Digit—all non-zero digits and zero when it has a non-zero digit to the left of it as in 4.03

IMPORTANT PROPERTIES

Commutative Property For Addition—the order in which numbers are added does not affect the sum

$$6 + 4 = 4 + 6$$

Commutative Property For Multiplication—the order in which numbers are multiplied does not affect the product

$$8 \times 3 = 3 \times 8$$

Associative Property For Addition—the way in which numbers are grouped does not affect the sum

$$7 + (3 + 2) = (7 + 3) + 2$$

Associative Property For Multiplication—the way in which numbers are grouped does not affect the product

$$(5 \times 2) \times 4 = 5 \times (2 \times 4)$$

Distributive Property—to multiply a sum of numbers, you can add the numbers and then multiply the sum

$$4 \times (6 + 3) = 4 \times 9 = 36$$

or you can multiply the numbers separately and then add the products

$$4 \times (6 + 3) = (4 \times 6) + (4 \times 3) = 24 + 12 = 36$$

Identity Property For Addition—the sum of zero and any number is that number

$$7 + 0 = 7 \qquad 486 + 0 = 486$$

Identity Property For Multiplication—the product of 1 and any number is that number

$$9 \times 1 = 9 \qquad 5840 \times 1 = 5840$$

Opposites Property—if the sum of two numbers is zero, then each number is the opposite of the other

$$-4 \text{ is the opposite of } + 4 \text{ because } -4 + (+4) = 0$$

Equation Properties—you can add or subtract the same number or multiply or divide by the same number on both sides of an equation and the result is still an equation

$$n - 6 = 7$$
$$n - 6 + 6 = 7 + 6$$
$$n = 13$$

$$4n = 24$$
$$\frac{4n}{4} = \frac{24}{4}$$
$$n = 6$$

WHICH MEASURE?

LENGTH

Metric System

1 centimeter (cm)	=	10 millimeters (mm)
1 decimeter (dm)	=	10 centimeters (cm)
1 meter (m)	=	10 decimeters (dm)
1 meter (m)	=	100 centimeters (cm)
1 meter (m)	=	1000 millimeters (mm)
1 decameter (dkm)	=	10 meters (m)
1 hectometer (hm)	=	100 meters (m)
1 kilometer (km)	=	100 decameters (dkm)
1 kilometer (km)	=	1000 meters (m)

U.S. System

1 foot (ft)	=	12 inches (in)
1 yard (yd)	=	36 inches (in)
1 yard (yd)	=	3 feet (ft)
1 mile (mi)	=	5280 feet (ft)
1 mile (mi)	=	1760 yards (yd)

AREA

Metric System

1 square meter (m²)	=	100 square decimeters (dm²)
1 square meter (m²)	=	10,000 square centimeters (cm²)
1 hectare (ha)	=	0.01 square kilometer (km²)
1 hectare (ha)	=	10,000 square meters (m²)
1 square kilometer (km²)	=	1,000,000 square meters (m²)
1 square kilometer (km²)	=	100 hectares (ha)

U.S. System

1 square foot (ft²)	=	144 square inches (in²)
1 square yard (yd²)	=	9 square feet (ft²)
1 square yard (yd²)	=	1296 square inches (in²)
1 acre (a)	=	4840 square yards (yd²)
1 acre (a)	=	43,560 square feet (ft²)
1 square mile (mi²)	=	640 acres (a)

VOLUME

Metric System

1 cubic decimeter (dm³)	=	0.001 cubic meter (m³)
1 cubic decimeter (dm³)	=	1000 cubic centimeters (cm³)
1 cubic decimeter (dm³)	=	1 liter (L)
1 cubic meter (m³)	=	1,000,000 cubic centimeters (cm³)
1 cubic meter (m³)	=	1000 cubic decimeters (dm³)

U.S. System

1 cubic foot (ft³)	=	1728 cubic inches (in³)
1 cubic yard (yd³)	=	27 cubic feet (ft³)
1 cubic yard (yd³)	=	46,656 cubic inches (in³)

CAPACITY

Metric System

1 teaspoon	=	5 milliliters (mL)
1 tablespoon	=	12.5 milliliters (mL)
1 liter (L)	=	1000 milliliters (mL)
1 liter (L)	=	1000 cubic centimeters (cm³)
1 liter (L)	=	1 cubic decimeter (dm³)
1 liter (L)	=	4 metric cups
1 kiloliter (kL)	=	1000 liters (L)

U.S. System

1 tablespoon (T)	=	3 teaspoons (t)
1 cup (c)	=	16 tablespoons (T)
1 cup (c)	=	8 fluid ounces (fl oz)
1 pint (pt)	=	2 cups (c)
1 pint (pt)	=	16 fluid ounces (fl oz)
1 quart (qt)	=	4 cups (c)
1 quart (qt)	=	2 pints (pt)
1 quart (qt)	=	32 fluid ounces (fl oz)
1 gallon (gal)	=	16 cups (c)
1 gallon (gal)	=	8 pints (pt)
1 gallon (gal)	=	4 quarts (qt)
1 gallon (gal)	=	128 fluid ounces (fl oz)

WEIGHT

Metric System

1 gram (g)	=	1000 milligrams (mg)
1 kilogram (kg)	=	1000 grams (g)
1 metric ton (t)	=	1000 kilograms (kg)

U.S. System

1 pound (lb)	=	16 ounces (oz)
1 ton (T)	=	2000 pounds (lb)

TIME

1 minute (min)	=	60 seconds (sec)	1 year (yr)	=	52 weeks
1 hour (hr)	=	60 minutes (min)	1 year (yr)	=	365¼ days
1 day	=	24 hours (hr)	1 decade	=	10 years
1 week	=	7 days	1 century	=	100 years

CAN YOU SPEAK METRIC?

pico	p	one trillionth
nano	n	one billionth
micro	M	one millionth
milli	m	one thousandth
centi	c	one hundredth
deci	d	one tenth
deka	da	ten
hecto	h	one hundred
kilo	k	one thousand
mega	M	one million
giga	G	one billion
tera	T	one trillion

MATHEMATICAL SYMBOLS

$ dollars

¢ cents

∅ empty set

[ ] empty set

% percent

π pi

$3.\overline{21}$ repeating decimal

45° (forty-five) degrees

F Fahrenheit

C centigrade

• point

√ square root

⌒ arc

÷ divide

⟌ divide

+ add

− subtract

× multiply

• multiply

∪ union of sets

∩ intersection of sets

= is equal to

≠ is not equal to

< less than

> greater than

≥ is greater than or equal to

≤ is less than or equal to

≈ is approximately equal to

~ is similar to

≅ is congruent to

+4 positive integer

−4 negative integer

— line segment

↔ line

→ ray

∠ angle

m∠ measure of angle

△ triangle

⊥ perpendicular

‖ parallel

5^3 exponent

ALL KINDS OF FORMULAS

Perimeter

$P = a + b + c$	Perimeter of a triangle
$P = 2(h + w)$	Perimeter of a rectangle
$C = 2\pi r$	Circumference of a circle

Area

$A = \pi r^2$	Area of a circle
$A = s^2$	Area of a square
$A = \frac{1}{2}bh$	Area of a triangle
$A = h\frac{(b_1 + b_2)}{2}$	Area of a trapezoid

Volume

$V = Bh$ (B is area of base)	Volume of a rectangular or triangular prism
$V = \frac{1}{3}Bh$ (B is area of base)	Volume of a pyramid
$V = s^3$	Volume of a cube
$V = \pi r^2 h$	Volume of a cylinder
$V = \frac{1}{3}\pi r^2 h$	Volume of a cone
$V = \frac{4}{3}\pi r^3$	Volume of a sphere

CONVERSION TABLES

From U.S. to Metric

U.S. Customary Unit	Approximate Metric Equivalent
inch	2.54 centimeters
foot	30.48 centimeters
yard	.91 meters
mile	1.6 kilometers
square inch	6.45 square centimeters
square foot	.093 square meters
square yard	.84 square meters
square mile	2.59 square kilometers
acre	4047 square meters
cubic inch	16.39 cubic centimeters
cubic foot	.028 cubic meters
cubic yard	.76 cubic meters
ounce	28.35 grams
pound	454 grams
ton	907.18 kilograms
pint	.47 liters
quart	.95 liters
gallon	3.79 liters
bushel	35.24 liters

And From Metric to U.S.

To change **centimeters**	to **inches**	multiply by **.3937**
To change **meters**	to **feet**	multiply by **3.2808**
To change **kilometers**	to **miles**	multiply by **.6214**
To change **liters**	to **quarts**	multiply by **1.0567**
To change **kilograms**	to **pounds**	multiply by **2.2046**
To change **metric tons**	to **tons**	multiply by **1.1023**

COMPUTER TALK

Basic - (Beginner's All-purpose Symbolic Instruction Code) a procedure-oriented computer programming language

Binary - a numbering system based on 2s that uses only two digits, 0 and 1; computers operate on a binary number system

Bit - one electrical signal (or one space that equals no signal) that combines with other bits to make computer codes; a binary digit

Bug - an error in the coding of a computer program

Byte - a term that measures binary digits; 8 or 16 bits

Chip - a tiny electronic component containing thousands of circuits

Cobol - (COmmon Business Oriented Language) a computer programming language

Computer - an electronic machine which stores instructions and information, deciphers and processes the instructions and information, performs tasks or calculations, and displays the "results" on a screen.

CPU - (Central Processing Unit) the part of the computer that performs logical processes

Data - information put into or received from a computer

Debug - to find and correct errors in a computer program

Disk - a thin, flat, circular metal plate with magnetic material on both sides used to store and read data

Disk Drive - a device in or attached to the computer which reads the information from the disks and stores the information

Floppy Disk - a flexible disk

Fortran - (FORmula TRANslator) a computer programming language used predominantly in science and engineering

Hard Disk - an inflexible disk

Hardware - computer machinery (such as the keyboard, disk drives, monitor, printer, and device containing the CPU)

Input - to enter data and instructions into a computer either manually or with computer input devices other than a keyboard

Interface - a connection between two computer systems or computer devices (such as the keyboard and the monitor or the printer and the computer)

Keyboard - a typewriter-like device with rows of keys which is used to type information into the computer

Memory - a device into which information can be stored

Microcomputer - a small, inexpensive computer system usually used in homes, schools, and small businesses

Monitor - a television screen which displays information

Output - information a computer displays on a screen or prints out after following a set of instructions or completing a task; information stored in memory or a computer file

Pascal - a computer programming language that emphasizes structured programming

PC - a personal computer, usually a microcomputer

Printer - a machine for printing output

Program - instructions given to a computer

Programmer - a person who prepares computer programs

RAM - (Random Access Memory) the part of a computer's memory that stores information needed for the computer to work properly (not available to the user)

Software - computer programs, usually found on disks, tapes, or cards

Terminal - a device for displaying input and output, usually located separately from the computer itself and generally consisting of a keyboard and monitor

MATH TERMS FOR EVERY OCCASION

Absolute Value - the distance a number is from 0 on the number line

Abundant Number - any number for which the sum of its factors (other than the number itself) is greater than itself

Addend - a number being added in an addition problem

In the equation 4 + 7 = 11, 4 and 7 are addends.

Addition - an operation combining two or more numbers

Additive Inverse - for a given number, the number that can be added to give a sum of 0

-4 is the additive inverse of + 4 because - 4 + (+4) = 0

Adjacent Angle - angles that have the same vertex and a common side between them

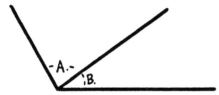

Angle A is adjacent to angle B.

Adjacent Side - the leg next to the given angle in a right triangle

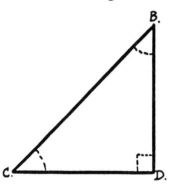

Side $\overline{CD}$ is adjacent to angle C.

Algorithm - a method commonly used for performing computations involving mathematical operations

Altitude of a Triangle - the distance between a point on the base and the vertex of the opposite angle, measured along a line which is perpendicular to the base (the altitude is also referred to as the height of the triangle)

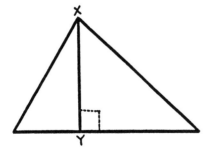

Segment $\overline{XY}$ is the altitude in this triangle.

Angle - a figure formed by two rays having a common endpoint (vertex)

An *acute angle* measures less than 90° (see # 1)

A *right angle* measures 90° (see # 2).

An *obtuse angle* measures more than 90° and less than 180° (See # 3).

A *straight angle* measures 180° (See # 4).

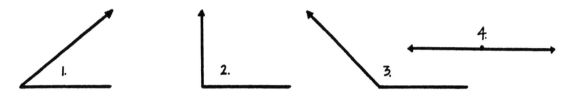

Central Angle - an angle formed by two radii of a circle.

Angle M is a central angle.

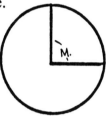

Complementary Angles - two angles whose combined measures equal 90°; X and Y (below) are complementary angles

Congruent Angles - angles having the same measure

Corresponding Angles - angles which are formed when a line intersects two parallel lines; corresponding angles are congruent; B and F (below) are corresponding angles

Supplementary Angles - two angles whose combined measures equal 180°; A and B (below) are supplementary angles

Vertical Angles - angles which are formed opposite one another when two lines intersect; vertical angles are congruent; E and H (below) are vertical angles

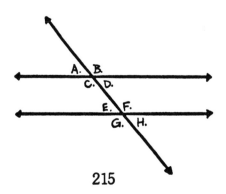

Arc - a part of a circle between any two points on the circle

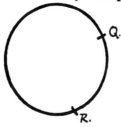

Segment $\overset{\frown}{QR}$ is an arc.

Area - the measure of the region inside a closed plane figure; area is measured in square units

Associative Property For Addition and Multiplication - the rule stating that the grouping of addends or factors does not affect the sum or product

$(3 + 6) + 9 = 3 + (6 + 9)$ $(2 \times 4) \times 7 = 2 \times (4 \times 7)$

Average - the sum of a set of numbers divided by the number of addends

The average of 1, 2, 7, 3, 8, and 9 = $\dfrac{1 + 2 + 7 + 3 + 8 + 9}{6}$ = 5

Axes - two perpendicular number lines with a common origin

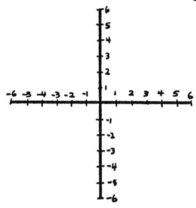

Axis - a number line which may be vertical or horizontal

Base - 1. a side of a geometric figure 2. a standard grouping of a numeration system

If a numeration system groups objects by fives, it is called a base 5 system (23 is a base 5 numeral meaning two fives and three ones).

Binary Operation - any operation involving two numbers

Bisect - to divide into two congruent parts

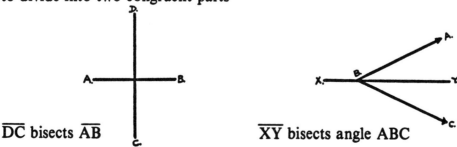

$\overline{DC}$ bisects $\overline{AB}$ $\overline{XY}$ bisects angle ABC

216

Bisector - a line or ray that divides a segment or angle into two congruent parts

Capacity - the measure of the amount that a container will hold

Cardinal Number - the number of elements in a set

Cartesian Set - a set resulting from the pairing of members of two other sets

Chance - the probability or likelihood of an occurrence

Chord - a line segment having endpoints on a circle

$\overline{XY}$ is a chord.

Circle - a closed curve in which all points on the edge are equidistant from a given point in the same plane

Circumference - the distance around a circle

circumference = π x diameter

Closed Figure - a set of points that encloses a region in the same plane; a curve that begins and ends at the same point

Coefficient - in the expression 8x, 8 is the coefficient of x

Coincide - two lines coincide when they intersect at more than one point

Collinear - when points are on the same line, they are collinear

Common Denominator - a whole number that is the denominator for both members of a pair of fractions

For $\frac{3}{7}$ and $\frac{5}{7}$, 7 is a common denominator.

Common Factor - a whole number which is a factor of two or more numbers (3 is a factor common to 6, 9, and 12)

Common Multiple - a whole number that is a multiple of two or more numbers (12 is a multiple common to 2, 3, 4, and 6)

Commutative Property for Addition and Multiplication - the rule stating that the order of addends or factors has no effect on the sum or product

$$3 + 9 = 9 + 3 \text{ and } 4 \times 7 = 7 \times 4$$

Compass - a tool for drawing circles

Complex Fraction - a fraction having a fraction or a mixed numeral as its numerator and/or denominator

$$\frac{\frac{2}{5}}{\frac{1}{3}}$$

Composite Number - a number having at least one whole number factor other than 1 and itself

Cone - a space figure with a circular base and a vertex

Congruent - of equal size and shape; the symbol $\cong$ means congruent

Triangles ABC and
DEF are congruent.

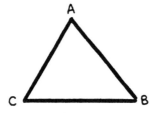 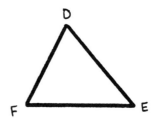

Coordinate Plane - a grid on a plane with two perpendicular lines of axes

Coordinates - a pair of numbers which give the location of a point on a plane

Coplanar - when lines or points are in the same plane, they are coplanar

Cross Product Method - means of testing for equivalent fractions

If $\frac{3}{5} = \frac{6}{10}$, then 3 x 10 will equal 5 x 6.

Cube - a space figure having six congruent, sqare faces

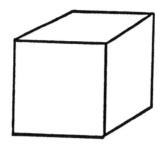

Curve - a set of points connected by a line segment

Customary units - units of the measurement system commonly used in a given country (inches, feet, pounds, ounces, and miles are customary units in the U.S.)

Cylinder - a space figure having two congruent, circular bases

Data - figures, facts or information

Decagon - a ten-sided polygon

Decimal Numeral - a name for a fractional number expressed with a decimal point, such as .27 (4.03 is a mixed decimal)

Decimal System - a numeration system based on grouping by tens

Degree - 1. a unit of measure used in measuring angles (a circle contains 360 degrees) 2. a unit for measuring temperature

Denominator - the bottom number in a fraction; the denominator tells how many parts there are in a whole unit

Diagonal - a line segment joining two nonadjacent vertices in a polygon

$\overline{AC}$ is a diagonal in this figure.

Diameter - a line segment which has its endpoints on a circle and which passes through the center of the circle

$\overline{LM}$ is the diameter
of this circle.

Difference - 1. the distance between two numbers on the number line 2. the result of subtracting the lesser from the greater

Digit - a symbol used to write numerals; in the decimal system, there are ten digits (0-9)

Disjoint Sets - sets having no members in common

Distributive Property for Multiplication Over Addition - the rule stating that when the sum of two or more addends is multiplied by another number, each addend must be multiplied separately and then the products must be added together

$$3 \times (4 + 6 + 9) = (3 \times 4) + (3 \times 6) + (3 \times 9)$$

Dividend - a number which is to be divided in a division problem

In the equation $7\overline{)63}$, 63 is the dividend.

Divisibility - a number is divisible by a given number if the quotient of the two numbers is a whole number

189 is divisible by 9 because 189 ÷ 9 is a whole number.

Division - the operation of finding a missing factor when the product and one factor are known

Divisor - the factor used in a division problem for the purpose of finding the missing factor

$$12\overline{)24}^{\,2} \quad \text{The divisor is 12.}$$

Dodecahedron - a space figure with 12 pentagonal faces

220

Edge - a line segment formed by the intersection of two faces of a geometric space figure

Elements - the members of a set

Empty Set - a set having no elements, also called a null set

 represents an empty set.

Endpoint - a point at the end of a line segment or ray

G is the endpoint of
this ray.

Equation - a mathematical sentence which states that two expressions are equal

$$7 \times 9 = 3 + (4 \times 15)$$

Equator - an imaginary line at 0 degrees latitude on the earth's grid

Equilateral - having sides of the same length

Figure ABC is an equilateral
triangle. All of its sides
are the same length.

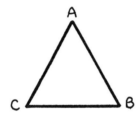

Equivalent Fractions - fractions that name the same fractional number

$\frac{3}{4}$ and $\frac{9}{12}$ are equivalent.

Equivalent Sets - sets having the same number of members

Estimate - an approximation or rough calculation

Even Number - one of the set of whole numbers having the number 2 as a factor

Expanded Notation - the method of writing a numeral to show the value of each digit

$$5327 = 5000 + 300 + 20 + 7$$

Exponent - a numeral telling how many times a number is to be used as a factor

In 6^3, the exponent is 3. $6^3 = 6 \times 6 \times 6 = 216$

221

Face - a plane region serving as a side of a space figure

Factor - one of two or more numbers that can be multiplied to find a product

In the equation 6 × 9 = 54, 6 and 9 are factors.

Factor Tree - a pictorial means of showing the factors of a number

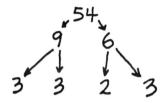

Finite Set - a set having a specific number of elements

$\{2, 5, 9, 15\}$ is a finite set.

Flip - to "turn over" a geometric figure; the size or shape of the figure does not change

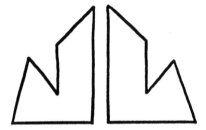

Fraction - the name for a fractional number written in the form $\frac{a}{b}$; a is the numerator, b is the denominator

Fractional Number - a number that can be named as a fraction, $\frac{a}{b}$; the numerator and denominator can be any numbers with the exception that the denominator cannot be 0

Frequency - the number of times a given item occurs in a set of data

Frequency Graph - a way to organize and picture data using a grid

Frequency Table - data arranged on a table to show how often events occur

Function - a set of ordered pairs of numbers which follow a function rule and in which no two first numbers are the same

$\{ (2,5) \ (3,6) \ (4,7) \ (5,8) \ (6,9)\}$ The rule for this set is to add one.

Geometry - the study of space and figures in space

Gram - a standard unit for measuring mass in the metric system

Graph - a drawing showing relationships between sets of numbers

Greatest Common Factor - the largest number that is a factor of two other numbers (6 is the greatest common factor of 18 and 24)

Grid - a set of horizontal and vertical lines spaced uniformly

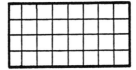

Hemisphere - half of a sphere

Heptagon - a seven-sided polygon

Hexagon - a six-sided polygon

Horizontal - a line that runs parallel to a base line

Line $\overleftrightarrow{GH}$ is a horizontal line.

Hypotenuse - the longest side of a right triangle located opposite the right angle

Side $\overline{OP}$ is the hypotenuse of this triangle.

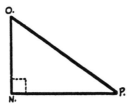

Icosahedron - a space figure with 20 faces

Identity Element For Addition - 0 is the identity element for addition because any number plus 0 equals that number

$$(3 + 0 = 3)$$

Identity Element For Multiplication - the number 1 is the identity element for multiplication because any number multiplied by 1 equals that number

$$(17 \times 1 = 17)$$

Improper Fraction - a fraction having a numerator equal to or greater than the denominator, therefore naming a number of 1 or more

$$\frac{9}{4} \text{ is an improper fraction.}$$

Inequality - a number sentence showing that two groups of numbers stand for different numbers

The signs $\neq$, $<$, and $>$ show inequality. $7 + 5 \neq 12 - 9$

Infinite Set - a set having an unlimited number of members

Integer - any member of the set of positive or negative counting numbers and 0

$$(\ldots -4, -3, -2, -1, 0, 1, 2, 3, 4, \ldots)$$

Intersection of Lines - the point at which two lines meet

Lines $\overleftrightarrow{AB}$ and $\overleftrightarrow{CD}$ intersect at point Y.

Intersection of Planes - a line formed by the set of points at which two planes meet

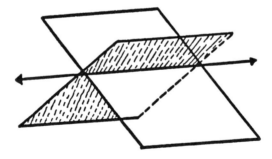

Intersection of Sets - the set of members common to each of two or more sets

The intersection of these sets is 3, 7, and 8. The symbol $\cap$ represents intersection.

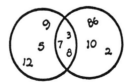

Inverse - opposite; addition and subtraction are inverse operations and multiplication is the inverse of division

224

Irrational Number - a decimal that neither terminates or repeats

Lateral Faces - the plane surfaces of a space figure which are not bases

The lateral faces of this
triangular prism are shaded.

Latitude - the distance, measured in degrees, north or south of the equator; lines of latitude run parallel to the equator

Least Common Denominator - the smallest whole number which is a multiple of the denominators of two or more fractions

The least common denominator for $\frac{1}{3}$ and $\frac{3}{4}$ is 12.

Least Common Multiple - the smallest whole number which is divisible by each of two or more given numbers

The least common multiple of 2, 6, 9, and 18 is 18.

Legs - sides adjacent to the right angle in a right triangle

$\overline{QP}$ and $\overline{QR}$ are legs
in this triangle.

Like Fractions - fractions having the same denominator

$\frac{2}{9}$ and $\frac{12}{9}$ are like fractions.

Line - one of the four undefined terms of geometry used to define all other terms

Line of Reflection - the Y-axis in a number plane

Line of Symmetry - a line on which a figure can be folded so that the two parts are exactly the same

Line $\overleftrightarrow{ST}$ is the line of
symmetry in this figure.

Line Segment - part of a line consisting of a path between two endpoints

$\overline{AB}$ and $\overline{CD}$ are line segments.

Linear Measure (or length) - the measure of distance between two points along a line

Liter - a metric system unit of measurement for liquid capacity

Longitude - the distance, measured in degrees, east or west of the prime meridian; lines of longitude run north and south on the earth's grid, meeting at the poles

Lowest Terms - when a fraction has a numerator and denominator with no common factor greater than 1, the fraction is in lowest terms

$$\frac{3}{7}$$ is a fraction in lowest terms.

Mean - average; the sum of numbers in a set divided by the number of addends

The mean of 6, 8, 9, 19, and 38 is $\frac{80}{5}$ or 16.

Measurement - the process of finding the length, area, capacity, or amount of something

Median - the middle number in a set of numbers; the median is determined by arranging numbers in order from lowest to highest and by counting to the middle

The median of (3, 8, 12, 17, 20, 23, 27) is 17.

Median of a Trapezoid - the line segment joining the midpoints of the nonparallel sides of a trapezoid

Meter - a metric system unit of linear measurement

Metric System - a system of measurement based on the decimal system

Midpoint - a point that divides a line segment into two congruent segments

Point B is the midpoint
of $\overline{DE}$.

Mixed Numeral - a numeral that includes a whole number and a fractional number or a whole number and a decimal

$7\frac{1}{2}$ and 37.016 are mixed numerals.

Mode - the score or number found most frequently in a set of numbers

Modular Number System - a number system that uses a limited number of units for counting

Multiple - the product of two whole numbers

Multiplication - an operation involving repeated addition

$$4 \times 5 = 4 + 4 + 4 + 4 + 4$$

Multiplicative Inverse - for any given number, the number that will yield a product of 1

$\frac{4}{3}$ is the multiplicative inverse of $\frac{3}{4}$ because $\frac{4}{3} \times \frac{3}{4} = 1$.

Napier's Bones - an early calculating tool, similar in principle to the slide rule, used for multiplication

Negative Integer - one of a set of counting numbers that is less than 0

Nonagon - a nine-sided polygon

Number - a mathematical idea concerning the amount contained in a set

Number Line - a line which has numbers corresponding to points along it

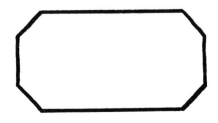

Numeral - a symbol used to represent or name a number

Numeration System - a system of symbols used to express numbers

Numerator - the number above the line in a fraction

Octagon - an eight-sided polygon

Octahedron - a space figure with eight faces

Odd Number - a whole number belonging to the set of numbers equal to (n x 2) + 1

(1, 3, 5, 7, 9 . . .) are odd numbers.

Odds Against - the ratio of the number of unfavorable outcomes to the number of favorable outcomes

Odds in Favor - the ratio of the number of favorable outcomes to the number of unfavorable outcomes

Open Sentence - a number sentence with a variable

Opposite Property - a property which states that if the sum of two numbers is 0, then each number is the opposite of the other

-4 + 4 = 0 ; -4 and 4 are opposites

Ordered Pair - a pair of numbers in a certain order with the order being of significance

Ordinal Number - a number telling the place of an item in an ordered set (sixth, eighth, etc.)

Origin - the beginning point on a number line; the origin is often 0

Outcome - a possible result in a probability experiment

Palindrome - a number which reads the same forward and backward

(343, 87678, 91219, etc.)

Parallel Lines - lines in the same plane which do not intersect

These lines
are parallel.

Parallelogram - a quadrilateral whose opposite sides are parallel

Pentagon - a five-sided polygon

Percent - a comparison of a number with 100

43 compared to 100 is 43%

Perimeter - the distance around the outside of a closed figure

Periods - groups of three digits in numbers

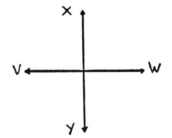

millions period   thousands period   units period

Perpendicular Lines - two lines in the same plane that intersect at right angles

These lines are
perpendicular to
one another.

Pi - the ratio of a circle's circumference to its diameter

pi = 3.14159265 (a non-terminating decimal)

The symbol π signifies pi.

Pictograph - a graph that uses pictures or symbols to represent numbers

Place Value - the value assigned to a digit due to its position in a numeral

Plane - one of the four undefined terms of geometry used to define all other terms

Plane Figure - a set of points in the same plane enclosing a region

Figures A and B are plane figures.

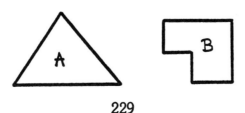

Point - one of the four undefined terms in geometry used to define all other terms

Polygon - a simple, closed plane figure having line segments as sides

Polyhedron - a space figure formed by intersecting plane surfaces called faces

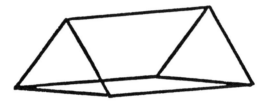

Positive Integer - one of a set of counting numbers that is greater than 0

Prime Factor - a factor that is a prime number

1, 2, and 5 are prime factors of 20

Prime Meridian - an imaginary line on the earth's grid located at 0 longitude which runs north and south through Greenwich, England

Prime Number - a number whose only number factors are 1 and itself

Principal - an amount loaned to someone or deposited in a bank

Prism - a space figure with two parallel, congruent polygonal faces (called bases); a prism is named by the shape of its bases

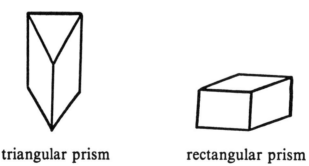

triangular prism   rectangular prism

Probability - a study of the likelihood that an event will occur

Product - the answer in a multiplication problem

Property of One - a property which states that any number multiplied by 1 will equal that number

Property of Zero - a property which states that any number plus zero equals that number

Proportion - a number statement of equality between two ratios

$$\frac{3}{7} = \frac{9}{21}$$

Protractor - an instrument used for measuring angles

Pyramid - a space figure having one polygonal base and four triangular faces which have a common vertex

Pythagorean Theorem - a proposition stating that the sum of the squares of the two shorter sides of a right triangle is equal to the square of the third side

In triangle ABC,
$\overline{AB}^2 + \overline{BC}^2 = \overline{CA}^2$

Quadrilateral - a four-sided polygon

 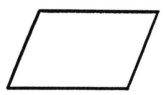

Quotient - the answer in a division problem

Radical Sign - the square root symbol

Radius - a line segment having one endpoint in the center of the circle and another on the circle

$\overline{FG}$ is the radius of
this circle.

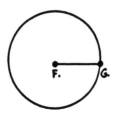

Random - an experiment in which the results are not predictable, even when repeated

Rate - a comparison of two quantities

Ratio - a comparison of two numbers expressed as $\dfrac{a}{b}$

Rational Numbers - a number that can be written as the quotient of two numbers (a terminating or repeating decimal is rational)

Ray - a portion of a line extending from one endpoint in one direction indefinitely

Real Numbers - any number that is a positive number, a negative number, or 0

Reciprocal Method For Dividing Fractions - a means of dividing fractions that involves replacing the divisor with its reciprocal and then multiplying

$$\frac{2}{3} \div \frac{4}{7} = \frac{2}{3} \times \frac{7}{4} = \frac{14}{12} = 1\frac{1}{6}$$

Reciprocals - a pair of numbers whose product is one

$$\frac{1}{2} \text{ and } \frac{2}{1} \text{ are reciprocals.}$$

Rectangle - a parallelogram having four right angles

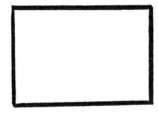

Region - the set of all points on a closed curve and in its interior

Relation - a set of ordered pairs

Remainder - the number (less than the divisor) that is left after a division problem is completed

$$
\begin{array}{r}
20 \\
21\overline{)426} \\
420 \\
\hline
6
\end{array}
\qquad 6 = \text{remainder}
$$

Rename - to name numbers with a different set of numerals

Repeating Decimal - a decimal in which a certain set of digits repeats without end (0.363636)

Replacement Set - a set of numbers which could replace a variable in a number sentence

Rhombus - a parallelogram having congruent sides

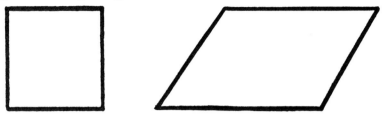

Roman Numerals - numerals used by the Romans for keeping records

Rounding - disregarding all digits in a number beyond a certain significance

Scale Drawing - a drawing of an object with all distances in proportion to the corresponding distances on the actual object

Scientific Notation - a number expressed as a decimal number (usually with an absolute value less than 10) multiplied by a power of 10.

$$4.53 \times 10^3 = 4530$$

Segment - two points and all of the points on the line or arc between them

Sequence - a continuous series of numbers ordered according to a pattern

Set - a collection of items called members or elements

Similarity - a property of geometric figures having angles of the same size

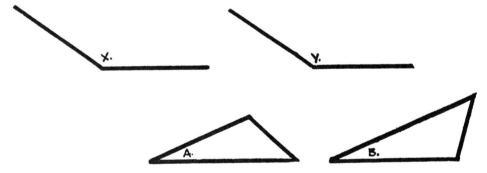

Angles X and Y are similar.   Triangles A and B are similar.

Simple Closed Curve or Figure - a closed curve whose path does not intersect itself

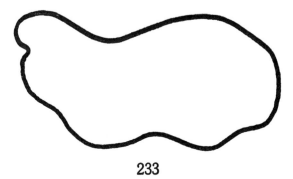

Skew Lines - lines that are not in the same plane and do not intersect

Skip Count - counting by skipping a certain number of digits (counting by 2s, 5s, and 10s, etc.)

Slide - moving a figure without turning or flipping it; the shape or size of a figure is not changed by a slide

Solution - the number that replaces a variable to complete an equation

Solution Set - the set of possible solutions for a number sentence

Space Figure - a figure which consists of a set of points in two or more planes

Sphere - a space figure formed by a set of points equidistant from a center point

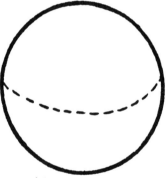

Square - a rectangle with congruent sides

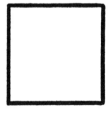

Square Root - a number which yields a given product when multiplied by itself

The square root of 25 is 5 because 5 x 5 = 25.

Statistics - numerical observations or data

Subset - every member of a set, or any combination of the members of a set

Subtraction - the operation of finding a missing addend when one addend and the sum are known

Sum - the answer in an addition problem resulting from the combination of two addends

Surface - a region lying on one plane

Surface Area - the space covered by a plane region or by the faces of a space figure

Symmetric Figure - a figure having two halves that are reflections of one another; a line of symmetry divides the figure into two congruent parts

These figures
are symmetric.

Tangent - a line which touches a curve at only one point

Line $\overleftrightarrow{GH}$ is tangent to the
circle at point X.

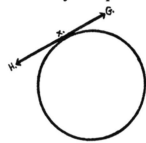

Terminating Decimal - a decimal that shows a quotient of a whole number and a power of 10

$$0.0204 = \frac{204}{10000} \qquad 3.56 = \frac{356}{100}$$

Terms of a Fraction - the numerator and denominator of a fraction

Tetrahedron - a space figure with four triangular faces

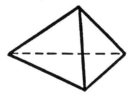

Transversal - a line that intersects two or more parallel lines

$\overleftrightarrow{GH}$ is a transversal of
lines $\overleftrightarrow{AB}$ and $\overleftrightarrow{CD}$.

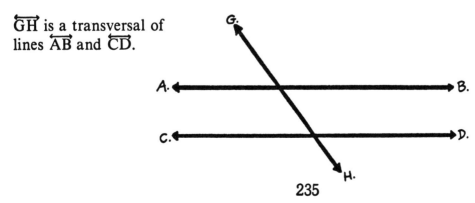

Trapezoid - a quadrilateral having only two parallel sides

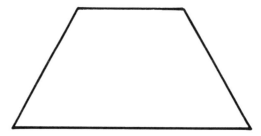

Triangle - a three-sided polygon

Acute Triangle - a triangle in which all three angles are less than 90°

Equilateral Triangle - a triangle with three congruent sides and three congruent angles

Isosceles Triangle - a triangle with at least two congruent sides

Obtuse Triangle - a triangle having one angle greater than 90°

Right Triangle - a triangle having one 90° angle

Scalene Triangle - a triangle in which no two sides are congruent

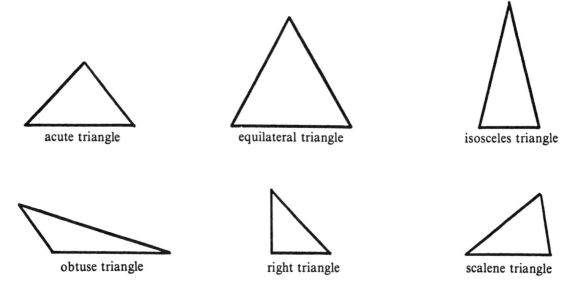

acute triangle   equilateral triangle   isosceles triangle

obtuse triangle   right triangle   scalene triangle

Turn - a move in geometry which involves turning, but not flipping, a figure; the size or shape of a figure is not changed by a turn

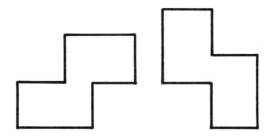

Union of sets - a set containing the combined members of two or more sets; the symbol ∪ represents union

The union of sets
A and B is
(7, 12, 14, 20, 26, and 25).

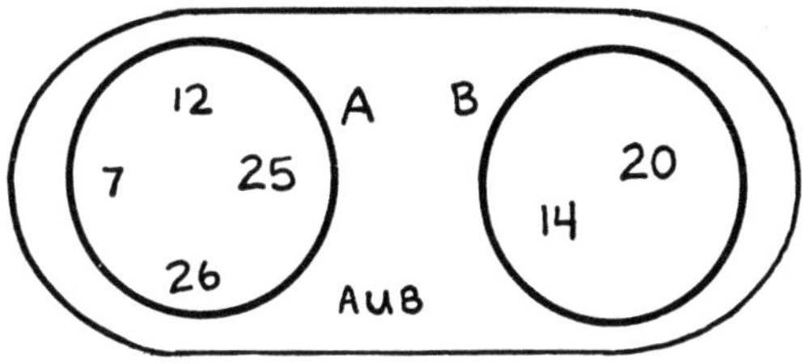

[Venn diagram: two overlapping circles labeled A and B inside an outer boundary. Left circle A contains 12, 7, 25, 26. Right circle B contains 20, 14. Labeled A∪B.]

Unit - 1. the first whole number 2. a determined quantity used as a standard for measurement

Variable - a symbol in a number sentence which could be replaced by a number

In $3 + 9x = 903$, x is the variable.

Venn Diagram - a pictorial means of representing sets and the union or intersection of sets (see example under Union Of Sets)

Vertex - a common endpoint of two rays forming an angle, two line segments forming sides of a polygon, or two planes forming a polyhedron

Point Z is the vertex
of this angle.

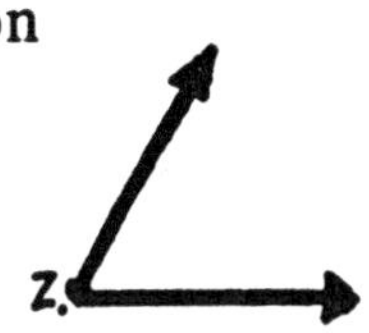

[Diagram of an angle with vertex labeled Z.]

Vertical - a line that is perpendicular to a horizontal base line

Line $\overleftrightarrow{KL}$ is vertical.

[Vertical line with arrows, labeled K at top and L at bottom.]

Volume - the measure of capacity or space enclosed by a space figure

Whole Number - a member of the set of numbers (0, 1, 2, 3, 4 . . .)

X-Axis - the horizontal number line on a coordinate grid

Y-Axis - the vertical number line on a coordinate grid

Zero - the number of members in an empty set

ANSWERS

Pg. 17 −4869, −3.9, −3, 3 1/2, 3.9, 56 1/10, 56 3/4, 5968, 75,000, 600,101, 601,099, 601,101

Pg. 19

306.25	8.108
306.2	8.08
21.055	7.906
21.005	1.003
2.105	0.0799
2.009	0.07969
0.109	0.079
0.100	0.032
0.009	

Pg. 21

A. distributive
B. distributive
C. associative
D. property of one
E. commutative
F. commutative
G. commutative
H. associative

Pg. 23 1.) 7 thousandths 2.) 9 tenths 3.) 5 hundred thousandths 4.) 9 ten thousandths 5.) 1 tenth 6.) 9 thousandths 7.) 3 thousandths 8.) 1 hundredth 9.) 4 ten thousandths 10.) 9 hundred thousandths

Pg. 27 1.) 61 2.) 401 3.) 168 4.) 1026 5.) 19 6.) 2694 7.) MCML 8.) LIV 9.) MMMCMXCVI 10.) CDXCIX 11.) LXXXVII 12.) MMMCDXCVIII

Pg. 32 1.) $105.37 2.) $400.75 3.) $12.80 4.) $1650.51

Pg. 34 about 9400 miles   **Pg. 39** 750,000   **Pg. 41** 10,000

Pg. 43 1.) 210 mph 2.) Elk 3.) Cheetah 4.) Spider 5.) Zebra or Greyhound 6.) Cheetah 7.) Elk 8.) Rabbit, Greyhound, Zebra, and Coyote 9.) Antelope is twice as fast as Grizzly 10.) Antelope

Pg. 49 $25.00   **Pgs. 52-53** Correct treasure: Video Gift Certificate

Pgs. 56-57 1.) Dorothy: 1200 2.) Slim: 0 3.) Dan: 1962 4.) Samantha 2,001,374 5.) Barb: 1974 6.) Muscles: 135 7.) Jake: 20 8.) Sally: depends on year 9.) Louise: 1640 10.) Pete: 0 11.) Sam: 110 12.) Ellie: 656

Pg. 59

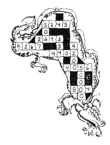

Pg. 60
1. 2,775,000,000
2. 80 yrs
3. Mars
4. 1,638,000,000
5. 2,723,000,000
6. Jupiter
7. About 85,775 days
8. Neptune

Pg. 62 1.) 473,000 2.) 10,036,519,800 3.) 2,968,900 4.) 2,729,800 5.) 6053.9007 6.) 1.0001 7.) 298.3400 8.) 88.6345 9.) 29,000 10.) 4000 11.) 800,444,000 12.) 123,456,789,000

Pg. 67 2/7, 1/3, 5/12, 4/9, 3/5, 7/10, 9/11

Pg. 73 New Recipe: 2 1/3 lbs. moth dust   2/3 iguana tooth
                       1 7/9 qt goblin grease   3 1/4 qt rat blood
                       1/6 C lizard scales   1 1/9 bat wings
                       14/15 C toad warts   1/3 vampire tongue
                       3 5/9 gal spider broth   1 5/6 C monster meat

Pg. 74 Bat Wing Stew

Pgs.   A) 6 2/5   B) 11/27   C) 5 11/21   D) 3 5/22   E) 1/330
76-77   F) 10 1/11

Pg. 84 a) .2$\overline{6}$ b) .1$\overline{6}$ c) .13$\overline{6}$ d) .08$\overline{3}$ e) .$\overline{2}$ f) .$\overline{6}$ g) .$\overline{407}$ h) .$\overline{3}$ i) .1$\overline{5}$ j) .$\overline{216}$

Pg. 85 Gold: Kayja (9.5)   Silver: Susan (9.3)   Bronze: Tyne (9.0)

Pg. 88 1.) Bigtooth   2.) 110.17 lbs.   3.) 63.75 lbs.   4.) 5.4 ft.   5.) Suzy: 16.67 lbs;
        Bigtooth: 26.78 lbs; Molars 34.28 lbs; Smiley: 43.89 lbs; Jaws: 6.43 lbs.

Pgs.   A.) 23.13   B.) 86.17   C.) 73.25   D.) 13.41   E.) 3.32   F.) 1.36
90-91   G.) 10.44   H.) 3.34   I.) 3.00   J.) 12.53

Pg. 95 1.) 9/20   2.) 1/10   3.) 13/20   4.) 12/25   5.) 0.9   6.) 0.55   7.) 0.3   8.) 0.6

Pg. 97 1.) $536.00   2.) 4   3.) 2464   4.) 52   5.) 3   6.) $102.00   7.) 115   8.) 322   9.) 2
        10.) 5

Pg. 101 1.) 23.3 ft.   2.) 34.9 ft.   3.) 11.7 ft.   4.) 7   5.) 15 days   6.) about 13

Pg. 102 #66--8   #26--15   #81--33   #40--20   #008--23

Pg. 103 F

Pg. 105 1.) 22% increase   2.) 4% decrease   3.) 71% decrease   4.) 3.5% increase
         5.) 16% increase   6.) 5% increase   7.) 11% increase   8.) 15% increase

Pg. 106 1.) 52   2.) 50   3.) 20   4.) 250   5.) 30

Pg. 110 1.) approx. 4.9 miles   2.) approx. 5.4 miles   3.) approx. 4.2 miles

Pg. 111 Portland: 800 mi; Juneau: 1200 mi; Salt Lake City: 1600 mi; Chicago: 1500 mi;
         Boston: 1300 mi; Atlanta: 1200 mi; Miami: 600 mi; Dallas: 1100 mi; Los Angeles:
         1400 mi; San Francisco: 400 mi

Pg. 121 1.) less   2.) more   3.) less   4.) more   5.) more   6.) less   7.) more   8.) less

Pg. 122 1.) 41 lb   2.) 163,380.66 lb   3.) 12 lb   4.) 144 lb   5.) 5 lb

Pgs.   1.) cubic cm.   2.) cubic cm.   3.) square m. (or liters)   4.) liters or kiloliters
126-127   5.) m.   6.) square cm.   7.) m.   8.) m.   9.) square cm.   10.) km.   11.) ml.   12.) kg.
          13.) square km.   14.) m.   15.) ml

Pg. 133 A.) line segment   B.) intersecting lines   C.) perpendicular lines
         D.) ray   E.) line   F.) angle   G.) parallel lines

Pg. 134 1.) M   2.) D   3.) G   4.) J   5.) B   6.) P   7.) A   8.) N   9.) L   10.) 0
         11.) C   12.) F   13.) K   14.) I   15.) H   16.) E

Pg. 140 1.) triangular prism   2.) cube or rectangular prism   3.) hexagonal prism
         4.) octahedron   5.) hexagonal pyramid   6.) square pyramid
         7.) triangular pyramid   8.) rectangular prism or cube

Pg. 141   sphere

Pg. 147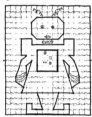

Pgs.   a) 1/2   b) 2/6 or 1/3   c) 2/7   d) 1/28   e) 1/2   f) 1/6   g) 3/5   h) 2/4 or 1/2
156-157   i) 1/4   j) 0   k) 1/6   l) 4/4

Pg. 161   1.) 108   2.) 98   3.) 102   4.) 47

Pg. 165   1) 1885-1886   2) 1889   3) 1887-1888   4) werewolf   5) 1885

Pg. 169   1) G   2) L   3) F   4) E   5) J   6) N   7) I   8) M   9) A   10) B   11)C   12) K

Pg. 171   1.) d = 12   2.) b = 888   3.) x = 7   4.) K = 11   5.) a = 471   6.) z = 5   7.) y = 1000

Pg. 178   1) Tom-4, Jamie-16   2) Katy-6, Mandy-12   3) Ramon-18, Jenny-3

Pg. 180   Clue: Frannie did not go to the reef. (Gayle--ships, Frannie--shark, Dan--reef, #3 is TRUE)

Pg. 181   1.) 55,019   2.) 25%   3.) 21,398   4.) 43,159   5.) 30,163   6.) 26,100 lbs.
           7.) Cleveland Stadium   8.) 5379

Pg. 184   1.) Usha-5 p.m.   2.) Sara-4 a.m. and Thomas-10 p.m.   3.) Ramon-6 a.m.
           4.) Sonja-3 p.m.   5.) Eduardo-7 a.m.   6.) Me Ling-8 p.m.   7.) Caroline-noon
           8.) varies

Pg. 187   1.) 16 cousins   2.) 7 aunts, 8 uncles   3.) 15   4.) 7   5.) 40

Pg. 189   1.) 36   2.) 50%   3.) .67 miles per min.   4.) 392 trips   5.) 56448   6.) 4900   7.) 150

Pg. 191   1.) #11   2.) #88   3.) #19   4.) #87   5.) #83

Pg. 194   1.) 86.7 seconds   2.) 17.143 seconds   3.) $1049.25   4.) 288   5.) 49/100

Pg. 195   Neon: Sleuth's Sandwich Shop;   King Kong: Wally's Waterbed Warehouse;
              capture jewel thief   discover submarine secrets
           Rocky Road: Snoop University;   Santa: Hideaway Hotel;
              find electronic brain   recapture ice cream formula
              (real agent 008)

Pgs.   A. 326   B. 1,679,616   C. 527   D. 200   E. 3777   F. 628   G. 2928
196-197   H. four

Pg. 198   1.) $24.46 (tip calculated with tax included)   2.) $3.42   3.) $8.55 more   4.) $1.28
           5.) $9.89 (figured with cup of minnow soup)

Pg. 200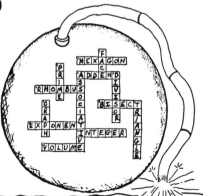